Secrets of Successful Fiction

SECRETS OF SUCCESSFUL FICTION

by Robert Newton Peck

Cincinnati, Ohio

The poem "Cat and Mouse" was excerpted from the book *Bee Tree and Other Stuff* by Robert Newton Peck. Text copyright 1975 by Robert Newton Peck, used with permission of the publisher, Walker and Company, New York.

Library of Congress Cataloging in Publication Data
Peck, Robert Newton.
    Secrets of successful fiction.
    Includes index.
    1. Fiction—Authorship. I. Title.
PN3355.P37   808'.025   80-14049
ISBN 0-89879-023-9
Book design by Barron Krody

Books by Robert Newton Peck

A Day No Pigs Would Die
Path of Hunters
Millie's Boy
Soup
Fawn
Wild Cat
Bee Tree
Soup and Me
Hamilton
Hang for Treason
Rabbits and Redcoats
King of Kazoo
Trig
Last Sunday
The King's Iron
Patooie
Soup for President
Eagle Fur
Trig Sees Red
Basket Case
Hub
Mr. Little
Clunie
Soup's Drum
Trig Goes Ape
Justice Lion

Dedication

I dedicate this book to Dr. Edwin Granberry.

When I was a student at Rollins College in Florida, he taught me all he knew about writing. He taught me all I know.

My teachers have carved my life.

Years ago, in a one-room schoolhouse in rural Vermont, my education began with Miss Kelly. For six years I was hers. And she was mine. A kid can't see God. Yet we saw Miss Kelly.

So, if Dr. Granberry will allow, I extend this dedication to all the teachers who ever taught me. Plus those who tried. To every teacher the world over, I want to say . . . thank you.

My gratitude runs deeper than words. If you read the books I wrote for children, you'll find a teacher-character in many of them. To name a few:

Miss Millerton in *Trig Goes Ape*
Miss Kelly in *Soup*
Mr. Little in *Mr. Little*
Miss Guppy in *Hub*.

In *all* my books for kids, the teacher stands tall. Often strict, yet always fair. And my kid-characters respect and honor their teachers, as the last chapter of *Soup and Me* will illustrate.

One evening a week, I teach a class in creative writing at Rollins College. And I'm proud to be a teacher. Not a Ph.D., but a *teacher*.

Years ago, Miss Kelly and Dr. Granberry handed me a lantern, to carry, and to cherish.

It was their dedication to me, and not this dedication that I now write to them, that will endure.

Robert Newton Peck

Contents

tool/Raise it to your mouth and yell/Look through it when you write/Zero in/One kid throwing one acorn at one turtle/Show one event in depth/Writing is a rifle, not a shotgun/Get yourself dirty/Crawl under a cow/Toot-ta-Doo

4. Two Dogs and One Bone 20
What's a plot?/Dramatic situations/Rover and Fido/Musical chairs/Make sure there is not quite enough to go around/To be alive is to want/What the savvy author must understand/Sex and violence/Corner the canines and define the prize meat/And the fur will fly

5. Nail Down the Camera 26
Opening night at the laundromat/Where's the camera?/Point of view/Who tells the story?/A trap to avoid/Multiple points of view/Only one camera/Tom Swift and his floating camera/Gnats on a rafter/Anchor your camera

6. Stay in the Phone Booth with the Gorilla 30
Alma was not alone/Nine gorillas in a phone booth/Quiet nights in Topeka/Doc Holliday's house call/Nothing but an old shoe/The beauty school in Valdosta/The gorilla nodded/Adhere to the here and now/Don't go gallivanting/Stick with the action

7. What's So Funny? 34
"Life's a junkyard"/Look for the daisies/Go visit a dump/Bask in a bit of beauty/A world of variety/Two hours of tuba honks is too much/ Two porters at the gate/What is Humor?/Laugh with others and laugh at yourself/Add a cello to your tuba

Introduction

This book is a toolkit for book builders.

Writing is not an art. It is a craft. And the more you work at it, the better you become. If you have the tools, and you know the secret of how to use them.

Trouble is, books on creative writing (except for this one) are often written by college profs who couldn't earn a penny as authors. They all have Chapter 1 of the great American novel tucked away in a bottom drawer, where it's been for twenty years.

So it's high time you switched from prof to pro.

Writing is a craft, like pottery making.

Without a potter's kickwheel, you won't turn out a pot. You need tools. This book of mine won't write that book of yours, but it will fill your kit with the tools of book building.

One thing this book is *not*, and that is a quick, surefire road to literary acclaim. Learning to write takes years, like becoming a doctor. So let's begin by signing you up for four years of college, four years of med school; with two more years of internship tacked on.

Ten years.

Is it worth it? You bet. Top authors work an hour or two a day and earn more money than most doctors. And have far more social status. Crowds beg for their autographs. People don't rush up to a doctor at a cocktail party to tell him that they read his latest X-ray.

Hard work is the secret.

Yet no builder, no matter how ambitious, can build a book without the proper tools. And my tools are simple to savvy.

Writing is not complicated.

It is a pig-simple craft that can be practiced using almost primitive utensils. On the college campi, prof after prof drones on to bored students about motivation, alliteration, punctuation . . . terms that don't mean much. Why do they do it? Because most college profs who teach writing were taught by their old profs who taught writing, who, in turn, were taught by Prince Valiant.

Nobody published anything. All they did was perpetuate hand-me-down myths, little sagas of academic jargon that created a few yawns, but few yarns.

I have a new name for campus creativity. It might be called *illiteration*.

This book was fun to write.

So I figure it will be fun for you to read. There's nothing in it to study, underline, memorize, or be quizzed on. Read it for pleasure. No desk necessary. It's an easy book for an easy chair.

Put your feet up, take your shoes and a Sunday off, and soak it in.

I won't build your book for you.

But you have a toolkit.

Get the Picture

Oh, go watch a radio!

Sound crazy? Sure, but that's what millions of Americans used to do, every evening before television came along. People used to sit for hours in their living rooms and stare at one little orange dial, watching a radio.

Why?

Because they wanted a picture. Not just voices. They wanted to *see* Amos and Andy, Fibber McGee, Lowell Thomas . . . the radio stars of yesteryear.

Readers of books are the same as watchers of radio. Readers want a *picture*—something to see, not just a paragraph to read. A picture made out of words.

That's what makes a pro out of an amateur. An amateur writer *tells* a story. A pro *shows* the story, creates a picture to look at instead of just words to read.

A good author writes with a camera, not with a pen.

The amateur writes: "Bill was nervous."

The pro writes: "Bill sat in a dentist's waiting room, peeling the skin at the edge of his thumb, until the raw, red flesh began to show. Biting the torn cuticle, he ripped it away, and sucked at the warm sweetness of his own blood."

The difference is obvious. A reader can't see *nervous.*
So make a picture. Instead of telling me that Bill is
nervous, show me Bill's thumb.

Here's another example.

The amateur writes: "The farmer had a horse and he
loved the horse very much and always took good care of
his horse."

Ho hum. No picture.

The pro might say: "Bending low, he hefted up her
massive hoof, to cradle gently between his knees as
though it were a child. As his hands worked the iron
tongs, he rubbed his head against the barrel of her side, to
quiet his mare from the pain."

Picture, picture, picture.

Whether you write adult novels or kiddie lit, the
process is the same. *Show*, don't tell.

Let's imagine that you're writing a story about two
kids: one narrates the story and another is very mean.

The amateur writes: "Janice was a very mean little girl,
who did mean things to me. I always hated Janice."

No picture.

The pro would write the following, not *telling* a reader
that Janice is mean, but *showing* it: "We were playing

Cowboys and Indians, and I was tied to a tree. Along came Janice. She yanked down my britches and chanted, 'I got a hornet.' "

That's a picture.

A pro is specific. His writing cites an example, instead of making a general statement. That example is usually a picture for a reader to see. Note, if you will, how TV replaced radio. People don't watch a radio anymore. They wanted a picture and that's what television offers.

Editors are people too. And, in case you don't already know how, here's how to bore an editor: Write a lot of sentences with no picture. Sentences like "John liked children very much."

A dandy little gem like that would even bore your mother. And she was the lady who used to look at the scrawls you lugged home from elementary school and tell you how wonderful they were.

Now then, if your mother is a Doubleday editor, you're all set. But if not, remember that *all* editors are people. And they don't relish reading manuscripts that are boring, boring, boring. So, instead of *telling* that John liked children, *show* it.

Like this:

John sat on a park bench, watching her skate toward him. He guessed her age at seven. When she came closer, he saw that one of her roller skates was loose. Around her neck, a rusty key hung from a dirty string. Smiling, he tightened her skate. Pulling a clean hanky from his pocket, he blotted a small scrape on her knee. As she skated away, he wondered why he had bothered. Until she turned, waved, and returned his smile.

Is there a picture?
Yes.

Now then, after you try to *show* instead of *tell*, how do you know for sure that you've made a picture? Easy. Just imagine that you are the artist who has been assigned to illustrate your book. (Even if it's a novel with no illustrations.) Are there frequent scenes in your manuscript that can be drawn? If not, then what you have written is dull, dull, dull.

Warning:

Sorrow, grief, and death are tough to handle, even for a pro. All emotions are difficult to write about. Love is, too. If you were writing a musical comedy for the theater, and you planned ten original songs, you'd find the hardest one to write was the ballad. The love song. Why? Because it's all been so often said.

So how do you handle emotion, a combination of love and sorrow?

With a picture.

Let's say a mother stands at a kitchen sink, washing the Saturday morning breakfast dishes. Johnny, her little boy, is ready to play baseball. Grabbing his baseball glove off the kitchen table, he starts for the door, but then gives her a quick swat on her behind with his glove.

To a mother, that one gesture is the Congressional Medal of Honor. A boy's way of saying, "Mom, you're an okay gal."

Now let's take this mother-son relationship a step further.

Years pass. Johnny didn't turn out so well. In high school he managed to get drunk, total a car, and get a nice girl pregnant. He got kicked out of the army and never could keep a job. His mother received a telegram that Johnny is dead. He died in a Mexican jail from an overdose of drugs.

The telegram she carries in her apron pocket. It has been unfolded, read, and refolded again and again.

She lives alone now. One evening, she goes upstairs

into the attic, to open up a dusty trunk. From beneath a pile of dingy quilts that have lost their color, she pulls out an old, dried, gritty hunk of leather. A baseball glove. Her hand, red and shiny from years at a sink, touches the thumb of the glove, where another, little hand had printed JOHNNY, a long time ago.

Closing the trunk, she slowly goes downstairs to sit in the dark parlor. Her rocker rocks, as she holds his baseball glove pressed softly to her breast.

Do you see a picture?

No words like *sorrow*, *grief*, *heartbreak* were used. Just an old woman and a baseball mitt. There were no tears rolling down her cheeks, no sobs.

One thing to remember about grief. Avoid putting tears in the eyes of your character. Instead, create a picture to bring tears to the eyes of your reader.

Do this, and you are a pro. Writing is not listing emotions. Writing is physics. Moving parts. Things.

Writing is *show* business. Get the picture?

How to Write Good with Swell Adjectives

Flowers belong in gardens, not in books.

As a reader, I can't stand flowery writing. A good author doesn't show off and slap in every pretentious word he knows. Writing is not description. It is action.

Writing is not a butterfly collection of adverbs and adjectives. Good fiction is a head-on crash of noun and verb. To me, a novel must be flat-footed, terse, and direct. So fire your words point-blank at close range. You'll bag a reader.

Here's what counts:

1. *Who* is in your book?
2. *What* does he do?

Please resist beginning your story with a description of the setting. This is the trademark of the amateur. Instead, start your book with a combination of talk and action. Nouns and verbs. If the book takes place in a small New England village, it is not necessary to list each building, from the marble bank to the white Congregational church.

Spare your reader the agony. He has already seen a small town and perhaps even lives in one. Or has in the past. And he's seen movies, watched television programs, and read books in which small towns abound.

What's going on?

That is the question that determines, to an anxious reader, the thrust and premise of your story. What's up? What's going down? What's coming off? What's *happening*?

I wrote a book (for kids) about spitting.

Its title is *Patooie*. The story unfolds in a small town which is never described. At least not by me. Yet, the town of Willetsberg is described by each and every character as they, one by one, enter the scene.

Chapter 1 opens with two boys busily engaged in boyish activity. A trivial task. Quincy and Hunk are trying to remove the cork disc from the belly of a beer-bottle cap. That's all. Just a bottle cap and a brace of boys.

The cork must be removed so that one of the boys can wear the PABST cap on his shirt, like a medal.

But then, out of the door of Spencer Webb's barbershop bursts Farly Palatka, a stout gentleman with shaving lather on his face, in a panic. The big seed-spit contest is only a day away, and Farly has just learned that the local champion, Mott Garland, has an infected tooth and can't spit.

The two boys enter the barbershop where, one by one, several of the town characters assemble to supervise Spencer Webb's extraction (in small towns, barbers sometimes doubled as dentists) of poor Mott's tooth.

Activity, not the author, depicts the town.

Even after the bothersome tooth is finally located and yanked, the physical condition of Mott's swollen mouth is not described. Instead, for the entire book, all Mott Garland can say is "Mfghxtzb."

No adjectives or adverbs are needed to color Mott's condition.

Only barber/dentist Spencer Webb's practiced ear can understand what Mott is saying, and he interprets the remarks to all concerned bystanders. A pretty girl walks by and Mott says "Mgzbtzh."

Spence adds, "She sure is."

When you write broadly, to create comedy, sometimes the *name* of your character serves to paint a rather vivid picture. (This ploy is used, of course, more in farce than in drama.)

Basket Case is a farce about teenage love and basketball. The apple of the hero's eye, Bathsheba Biltmore, is a leggy lass who is captain of the cheerleaders. Her name is enough to describe, for any reader whose glands yet function, her obvious charms. And her character.

No adjectives are needed to nail down her contours or construction. And no adverbs are needed to describe how the hero, Higbee Hartburn, longs for her.

Names are fun.

Not all editors cotton to weird names. Nor do all readers. I have learned that humor has its limitations. Punch lines you may deem a riot, others will spurn as dull, or strained. Comedy has a far more limited audience than drama. To succeed, an author has to discover a flock of followers with his identical funnybone.

The funniest book I ever wrote (in my opinion) was turned down by Knopf, Doubleday, and Little, Brown. Its title is *Orly's Sub*. It's a book about football, and someday they'll all be sorry and beg my forgiveness. But I won't give it to them. Never.

When this happens to you, don't get sore. Even if I did.

Just keep sending the doggone manuscript to other publishers and eventually you may hit it lucky. You'll stumble across an editor who twigs to the same brand of humor. And while the book is being considered, or rejected, write another one. Write the new novel on an entirely different subject, and on a fresh emotional level.

Whether you choose to create comedy or drama, the advice is the same.

Writing is not based on inert description. The description must be kinetic. Make it energetic. Active. Verbal, in the sense that verbs are action words. If you have a friend whom you hold dear, it is not because of what he or she is, but rather what he or she *does*.

I don't want an adjectival friend. I want a substantive pal.

And when I read a book, I look for that very same measure of value. The authors that I admire, and copy, are writers who activate a scene instead of describing it.

Yet there should be, in a mature novel, a meat-potato balance of a hero's reflections along with his deeds. When I was a soldier in World War II, at the farm-fresh age of seventeen, there were duties to perform as an infantry machine gunner. Yet, so much to think about too. Bullets and dreams.

Mostly, we talked about back home.

I shared Vermont with a corporal from Mississippi, Both our farms were such a long way from Italy that we became neighbors. As if his meadow and mine were separated by a single rail of fence.

We described not what our homes looked like, but who

was back there waiting . . . and the chores we did there. Dirty work, we prayed that we would do again.

Look Through a Toot-ta-Doo

Do you know what emerging writers do?

If they have to write three pages for an assignment, they try to tell the entire history of Valdosta, Georgia . . . and a bit about everyone who ever lived there or even passed through the town.

Reading those three pages is sort of like trying to plow with a blind mule. You never know where you are or where you're going.

Don't do it. Don't write like that. Zero in.

So stop right now, put this book of mine down, and do yourself a favor. Because there's a handy little tool (that you already own) that I beg you to add to your toolkit.

Go to your bathroom. Yank off all the toilet tissue from the roller and tell me what's left on the spool. It's the core. A little gray (or white) cardboard cylinder that's inside every roll of john paper, and it ought to have a name.

It's a Toot-ta-Doo. Because you can raise this tube to your mouth and yell "Toot-ta-Doo!" through it.

Big deal.

But save it. Look through it every time you write. No, you won't see much. Only a little round spot of something at the end of the tunnel. Yet whatever you choose to look at, through your little gray scope, you will zero in on. And write about in depth.

You won't see all of Valdosta.

What you *will* see is . . . one kid throwing one acorn at one turtle.

One pair of hands darning one sock.

One marshmallow being roasted at the end of one twig, over one little campfire.

Keep your Toot-ta-Doo with you. I'm serious. Continue to look through it and see not many things but one event in depth. Your writing will blossom with tone and texture.

Writing is not a shotgun.

It's a rifle.

You will soon be able to *show* your reader . . . one little girl catching one firefly in one jar.

And you'll quit, thank Heaven, *telling* me that Nature in the meadow is beautiful. You will *show* me one butterfly landing on one bluet. One drop of morning dew that clings to one strut upon the web of one spider.

Your friends will, of course, think that you're out of your tree. You've gone bonkers. Flipped. Maybe. But who publishes *their* stuff?

Ever take a walk in the woods?

A lot to see, huh? Too much. So get down on your belly, crawl around under a stand of brush, until you discover something that moves. It's alive. Watch it, and follow it to see where it's going. Like all living creatures, it seems to know where to go and what to do when it gets there.

Study it through your Toot-ta-Doo.

No, you won't see all of the meadow; and thank the good golly you won't *write* about all of it either.

You'll zero in.

And you'll stop informing me that "A bird flew over your head."

A bird? What kind of a bird was it? A giant California condor with an eight- or nine-foot wingspan? A shiny black raven? A hummingbird?

Get yourself dirty.

Crawl under a bush, a cow, an old car, and *show* me what you see. Share with me how such a discovery made you feel.

Your good pants may get rumpled, and Ludlow (whom you will meet in Chapter 9) may never forgive you, but getting yourself a tad grimy will bring you a tad closer to becoming a pro writer. Each hunk of dirt is a heap of help.

Before I wrote *Fawn*, I sure stumbled around through a lot of the forest that half-surrounds Fort Ticonderoga.

I had to see the French lines, the trenches that were cut by General Montcalm in that long-ago July. And later, inside the fort itself, I stood on the stone battlements looking toward the same trees . . . wondering what some young French soldier wondered. How many Black Watch (Scottish Highlanders) were advancing, bayonets fixed?

I heard the advancing bagpipes and this hiss of a Mohawk arrow.

It is 1758, I am but eighteen, and long to be home in France and milking our cow, Eugenie . . . feeling the silky warmth of her great side as I rest my head upon her flank.

Do I drop my musket and hear the clatter of its iron as it hits the gray stone at my feet?

When you become an author, someone who has read your book will come up to you and say, "As I read that battle scene, I felt as though I was really *there*."

To achieve this, a writer must see one soldier, with one musket, during one moment in his young life. To zero in is half the battle. So sound the charge.

Don't blow it. Look through it.

Toot-ta-Doo!

Two Dogs and One Bone

What's a plot?

A plot is two dogs and one bone.

Pig simple. That's all there is to it. A plot is merely a dramatic situation where a character

1. Wants something.
2. Tries to get it.
3. And is opposed.

Rover has a bone. Fido wants it. But if Fido never tries to take the bone away from Rover, we don't have much action. And if Fido tries to take the bone and friendly old Rover hands it over without even a snarl, we don't have a plot.

We have a dramatic situation only when Fido wants Rover's bone, tries to get it, and is opposed . . . because hungry Rover fully intends to keep his hunk of horsemeat for himself.

Have you ever played musical chairs?

Ten people, nine chairs. The music starts and everyone walks around the chairs in a circle. When the music suddenly stops, everyone tries to plant himself in a chair. It wouldn't be much of a game if there were ten people and ten chairs. The climax of the game is two fannies and one chair. Two dogs and one bone.

Not-quite-enough-to-go-around has been the basis for many a plot. Somebody wants something *that belongs to someone else.*

Two armies and one fort. One army occupies the fort (the bone) and the other army plans to storm it, take it, and shoo away the losers.

Cavalry and Indians and Little Big Horn. Bob and Bill and Daphne Delicious. Agnes and Alice and Mr. Henry Handsome. Fido, Rover, bone.

The bone is the pivotal issue. The bone is what's at stake. What's up for grabs.

Harwood Industries is a giant corporation headed by four men: an elderly chairman, a weak president unfit to take command, and two ambitious vice-presidents who want control of this corporation so much that they would eat their own young to get it. They want the salary, the stock, the power that being a chairman offers.

This, obviously, is a slight variation from Fido and Rover, as neither VP has the bone already in his fangs. But both pups McDermott and Lowe are drooling.

For fun, let's give our quartet some names.

Chairman   Graham Kenton Harwood (old)
President   Henry Paterno (weak)

VP   J. Allen McDermott (strong dog)
VP   Nancy Lowe (strong dog)
   Ah!

You noticed something, didn't you? One of the vice-presidents is a woman. Which means another spicy little herb has been added to your stew.

We already know Ms. Lowe is bright, as she is one of the two contenders for the crown. Is she also attractive? Is she married or single? Does she date? If so, whom? And does Harwood or Paterno or McDermott think of her in a personal way?

A dramatic situation, as we concluded earlier, is when somebody wants something.

Now, in the above plot about Harwood Industries, we see that a number of somebodies may want a number of things. There is more than one bone.

It boils down to *want*.

Mother Nature, in her wisdom, created all living things to *want* something. To be alive is to want, to seek, to get. Life is greedy. The talons of a hungry hawk extend to grab a rabbit as tree roots extend to grab earth. All of life has been ordained to be predatory. Even a carrot, one orange talon that stabs deep into soil, seeking and wanting that which is not yet its own.

So much for philosophy.

The *want*-syndrome is observed, understood, and practiced by every savvy author.

Meanwhile, back at El Rancho Harwood, who wants Ms. Lowe? And what does she desire? Or whom?

Consider the history of your characters. Ask yourself if Nancy Lowe was in love with McDermott, or he with her, a few years back? Was their love affair practiced in secret, or was it known by every other key member of the Harwood Industries brass?

So much for love.

Let's move on to hate. Who hates whom? And why?

With a prize as tasty as a chairmanship, somebody surely is bound to dislike someone.

One dog will get the bone. And, if we have a winner, this means that there must be a loser. A good loser? A poor loser? A loser who won't accept defeat? More fire to heat your stewpot to a merry bubble.

Money, love, hate, defeat, victory. Once you begin to cook, my how the recipe grows. Each element adds its own kindling to make the sparks fly.

Paterno, the weak president, interests me. He knows that Fate will not grace him with the crown of chairmanship. Yet he may have the deciding vote. Not a king but a kingmaker.

Is illness a factor?

Just how old and how sick is the current ramrod, G. K. Harwood? Perhaps all that is left for this old man is to slyly look down into the pit and watch the dogs scrap over the bone. Maybe he decides that what he will do is—absolutely nothing. Delay the contest. Drag it out for his own amusement.

Notice this, please: We have created a plot for a novel by using neither sex nor violence.

"Hold on!" you may be hollering. "You mentioned sex."

Wrong. Sex has not been mentioned. Only love. Certainly not pulp-mag sex, which won't add anything to this novel, and might even detract from it. If there is love, let it please have dignity.

Now for violence:

All clashes do not involve swords, guns, and karate chops. We don't need them here. Corporate executives may pose as gentlemen; but in this novel, they could kick, bite, and scratch with more ferocity than the Pittsburgh Steelers.

I have a hunch that Mean Joe Green of football fame may be Caspar Milquetoast compared to a certain Graham

Kenton Harwood. After all, G. K. didn't get where he got by being an Eagle Scout.

Just an eagle.

Thus we create the many pit dogs and the varied bones of discontent. How easy it is to plot a novel, once we corner the canines. And define the prize meat.

It's a lot like musical chairs. Make sure you have more dogs than bones.

And the fur will fly.

Nail Down the Camera

How do emerging writers write?

Without viewpoint. Amateur writers (who write with all the excitement of opening night at a laundromat) don't seem to know the first rule about viewpoint. So here it is in a nutshell.

You must ask yourself . . . "Where's the camera?"

That's all *point of view* means . . . it's just knowing where the camera is that records the action, dialogue, and thoughts.

Point of view is determined when the author decides who is going to tell the story. *Who* means which character. Or characters.

Some novels are written from the hero's point of view. His name is Hank Hero, and the camera is always inside Hank's handsome head. This applies whether the book is in first person or third. (Please avoid writing in second person.)

With the camera inside Hank, the reader learns what *all* the characters in Hank's presence are saying and doing. The camera also records the thoughts and feelings of Hank, *not* the thoughts or feelings of anyone else. Nailing down the camera, inside Hank's head, helps the reader feel Hank's pleasure or pain.

Here's a trap to avoid:

If you decide to write your novel only from Hank's viewpoint, Hank *must* be present in all scenes. You cannot write in a scene between Jack and Jill when Hank is off on a business trip to Topeka, checking in at the Morbid Motor Inn.

Hank is in every frame, and the camera in his head is merrily cranking away to record what *everyone* (including Hank) says and does.

Plus what Hank Hero *thinks*. We never know what any of the other characters think until they *say* or *do* something.

Next question:

Does the camera always, in every book, have to be in just one person's head?

No.

To write a book in which your characters think secret thoughts about each other, you must use multiple viewpoints, with the camera inside the heads of many. But remember this:

There's only *one* camera.

Chapter 1 may be written with the camera inside Hank. Chapter 2, in Jack . . . and now it records what *everyone* says and does; plus what Jack says, does, *and* thinks. Chapter 3, the camera is inside Jill.

Now then, this nifty little game of hot potato with a camera being passed around from head to head can be fun. Such a structure creates many possibilities.

Perhaps in your novel, Chapter 4 and Chapter 7 and Chapter 10 are all conversations between Jack and Jill. Chapter 4, the camera is in Jack. Chapter 7, in Jill. And in Chapter 10, in Hank, who's spying through a bedroom keyhole, hearing and seeing what Jack and Jill are saying and doing.

(I never did trust Hank.)

Best you flip your coin early on. Or you'll flip your lid.

By that, I mean that an author must, before the novel begins, decide: Is the camera to be in one character's head throughout? Or will it be a hot potato, changing heads from chapter to chapter?

I repeat. If old Hank is to be present in all important scenes, then and only then can Hank hold the camera for the entire book. If not, play hot potato. Switch viewpoints.

Which brings up another vital point.

In a hot-potato novel, where the viewpoint shifts, if Jill holds the camera in Chapter 1, keep it there for the entire chapter. Please. I beg you. Don't let the camera go floating off somewhere, or slip through a keyhole.

If there is one kind of writing that's boring to read it's *Tom Swift and His Floating Camera.*

Do *not* put the camera in the eye of a gnat up on a rafter who looks down and tells us what *everyone* says, does, and thinks.

Be *inside* somebody.

Anchor your camera. Nail it down. Put the pesky contraption in Jack's or Jill's or Hank's head and leave it there for an entire chapter.

When the camera is inside Jill, we readers get to know

her, to share her emotions, and eventually to like her. Or hate her. Especially the way she carried on with Jack when good old Hank was in Topeka.

(I never trusted *her*, either.)

Here's a problem. Can your camera ever go off to Topeka with Hank?

Sure it can.

It's your book. So if Hank skips off to Topeka, because that's where Mildred lives, then best we pack the camera along. How else can we cast a scornful eye at Mildred?

In fact, in a hot-potato novel with shifting viewpoints, Chapter 13 might be told through Mildred's eyes, recording what Hank says and does in Topeka, as well as everything that Mildred says, does, and *feels*.

I want you to read two of my novels. One is called *Eagle Fur* and it is told from one viewpont: Abbott Coe's. The other is *The King's Iron* in which the point of view changes from chapter to chapter. But the camera is *always* in *somebody*.

Never up in a rafter! Unless, of course, your hero is a termite.

Stay in the Phone Booth with the Gorilla

Your novel begins . . .

Alma walked hurriedly down the dark and deserted street. Hearing footsteps echo behind her, she darted into a telephone booth. Before closing the door, Alma Glook knew she was not alone. With her in that phone booth was a five-hundred-pound gorilla.

"Help!" yelped Alma.

Seeing the gorilla, her thoughts turned back in time to when she was a little girl, back home in Topeka, living with her Aunt Mildred who was a taxidermist and scratched out their meager living by stuffing gorillas. In fact, her aunt had earned quite a reputation in college when she had, as a prank, stuffed nine gorillas into a phone booth.

How clearly Alma recalled their little white cottage, modest but cozy, and the traveling salesman, Hank Handsome, who came to their door one May, selling Fuller brushes.

"Nothing," her Aunt Mildred had always told her, "can groom a gorilla as well as a Fuller brush."

Evenings were quiet in Topeka. The three of them (Aunt Mildred, Hank, and Alma) would stroll down to the drugstore to buy Alma a copy of *Jack and Jill*.

On Thanksgiving, instead of a turkey, Aunt Mildred would stuff a gorilla.

Christmas came, and Uncle Hank (as she was told to call him) gave both Alma and Aunt Mildred a Fuller brush.

Years passed.

Yet the brushes never stopped coming, due to Uncle Hank's boundless generosity. Even their two dogs, Fido and Rover, got a brush. To fight over.

As good old Uncle Hank's visits to Topeka became more and more frequent, he stopped staying at the Morbid Motor Inn, bunking in at the cozy little cottage.

One night, at the stroke of twelve, little Alma slipped silently from her bed to tippytoe down the hall and peek through Aunt Mildred's keyhole.

Her aunt and Uncle Hank were having a spat over the fact that Uncle Hank snored. Aunt Mildred threw a Fuller brush, which missed Uncle Hank but hit the keyhole, poking a bristle or two into Alma's eye.

The pain was intense. Worse than the toothache she'd suffered when old Doc Holliday made his first house call, prior to a gunfight.

Speaking of gunfights, Westerns were Alma's favorite

type of movie. Those, and Tarzan movies that featured a gorilla.

Spring arrived late. And her Aunt Mildred threw an Easter party, an egg hunt. Oh, how her aunt loved to watch the eager little faces of the neighborhood children as they poked under every bush and hedge, finding nothing but an old shoe. Years later, Alma learned that her loving aunt had hidden no eggs at all.

"You're rotten," Alma finally said.

Rotten?

Wasn't that the word that Aunt Mildred had called Uncle Hank the night she'd had it with his snoring? At least that was the picture in Alma's mind.

Uncle Hank left for Chicago.

Alma had never seen Chicago, but she had been to Valdosta, Georgia, which was almost the same. Valdosta was where Alma enrolled in beauty school, to become a manicurist, in order to eventually star in TV dishwashing commercials . . . like her other aunt, Madge.

For fun, Alma started writing for television, which led to her first novel, a biographical study of a young girl entitled *I Was a Hot Potato in Topeka.*

Writing came hard for Alma.

Night after night, she would pace the floor of her lonely room which was crowded, because she had brought along both Fido and Rover, three stuffed gorillas, and a five-hundred-pound Fuller brush.

Often she would take midnight strolls on the dark and dingy streets of Valdosta, passing phone booth after phone booth, wondering if she would ever see Uncle Hank again.

She loved him when he'd gotten dressed up, one Halloween, in a gorilla suit.

How much he enjoyed wearing his gorilla costume. He wore it more and more; even when he went door to door, selling Fuller brushes. That was when his sales started to slip. And the company gave him a pink slip, which he wore inside his gorilla costume.

And now, here she was, trapped in a phone booth with a gorilla.

"Uncle Hank?" she asked hopefully.

The gorilla nodded.

What's the point of this chapter?

Don't let Alma go off to Topeka. A writer must learn to stick to the *here-now* of an established situation, and not go gallivanting off to Topeka, Valdosta, or Flashback, Wyoming.

Please don't go to jail, or pass "Go," òr collect $200.

Diversions destroy the pace of a novel; and writers must, more rather than less, adhere to the action. Keep your story moving. It has been my observation that the emerging writer tends to wander off too often. Flashbacks are allowed, but insert them only when your hero is at ease, and in a thoughtful or nostalgic mood. Not during a scene of dramatic excitement.

I teach an evening course in creative writing. This allows me to see, once a week, about two dozen papers that leave Alma and the gorilla and meander off to Topeka, to the childhood of a local dentist, or to the inner workings of a jet engine. While poor Alma has to fend for herself. Amateurs, for some reason, feel compelled to tell all they know. Even if the reader doesn't want or need to hear it. What readers want to find out is whether or not Alma is getting gorilla'd in the phone booth.

Please don't wander. Stick with the action that you have taken the time and trouble to establish.

Stay in the phone booth with the gorilla.

What's So Funny

I once knew a kid named Jim.

It was a few summers back when I was teaching a course in creative writing at Manhattanville College in Purchase, New York.

Jim was twenty.

Yet everything he wrote read as if he were a hundred years old, blind, deaf, and disabled. Jim's manuscripts (two or three pages) were dark, dank, and totally negative. So after I'd received several doses of his dungeon diction, we had a chat.

"Why?" I asked him.

"Man," he said, "life's a junkyard."

"Okay," I said, "life *is* a junkyard. But I used to work in a junkyard. And in May, up through the jagged holes of rusty fenders daisies would grow. Yellow and white and beautiful. Plus you could faintly hear the merry squeals of young mice playing in the rubbish."

So when you write a book, my advice to you is to put some daisies in the junkyard.

If you don't dig junkyards, go visit a dump. It's amazing what people pitch out. Things with color and character. Like an old mattress that's half burned, losing stuffing, with broken and twisted springs.

7.

But once, a long time ago, that very mattress was new. A young bride selected it. She and her groom lugged it into a new home, where the mattress began to share a new life.

The mattress cradled lovers, and perhaps was a nest for the birth of a baby. For many a night that mattress rested the weary body of a worker who had sweated all day. And years later, an old man took sick and died on that bed.

The sweet daisies of imagination can grow just about anywhere, so let's bask in a bit of beauty.

What, by the way, is beauty? I'll tell you.

Beauty is variety.

God created for us a world of variety. We all are different—bugs, birds, fish, flowers, and folks. So you must vary your work. It can't be all the same hue and be a work of art.

Would you write a symphony that was two hours of tuba honks?

No. You'd bring in the flights of strings and the soft purr of woodwinds. Brassy trombones and trumpets, thunderous drums, cymbal crashes, and the tiny ting of a triangle.

Shakespeare used humor as a change of pace.

In *Macbeth*, in which there are several gory murders, Will Shakespeare broke up the blood by a comic scene: two oafish and drunken porters knocking at a gate at midnight. How come? The playwright knew that his play, his dramatic symphony, would be a ho-hummer if one murder followed the next. All tuba honks.

I borrowed that very idea.

Hang for Treason is a heavy book, about war and death. Which is why I chose to introduce a comic character, the Widow Starr, plus her brood of nubile daughters.

Here is a sample:

"Cussed animal," she yelled. "We're bound for Skenesboro, now that the road's dry."

According to Papa, the Widow Starr had learned to whisper in a sawmill. The beller of a bull was near to silence compared to every letter that passed her lips. Getting to her feet, our small and birdlike neighbor rubbed her backside, and let out a big sigh. Her daughters, all six of them, leaped lightly to the ground. They sure wasn't the plainest gals in Verdmont, looked at as a bunch.

"Morning, folks," screamed the Widow. "Say *good morning*, girls. Cat got your tongue?"

"Morning," the girls said in a chorus.

"Cream of the crop," hollered Widow Starr, "and every one a peach. You know my girls, don't cha, Able?"

"Yes'm."

"Propagate, Fruitful, Comfort, Ardent, Mingle and Nocturnal," she rattled off in full voice, as she always did on every visit. "Nocturnal means an animal that's active at night," she said, winking in my direction.

"Morning, all," said Papa, holding the horse.

"That son o' yourn," she screamed at my father

but looked my way, "is reached high time to produce a brood for himself. Ought to git that boy wedded and bedded."

The red in my cheeks was bubbling up for fair, and I did my best to think of some way I could change the subject. But I don't guess that a widow with six unwed girls of an age to marry could stand by and see ripe go rotten. Since I turned thirteen, almost five years back, the Widow Starr had begun my courtship with all half-dozen of her daughters, stopping by the house almost every month to see if I was ready to pick or choose.

"Ought to hear them girls o' mine recite the Bible," yelled Mrs. Starr with a nod of her head as a cue.

"Thy two young breasts are like two young roes that are twins, which feed upon the lilies," said Ardent.

"Songs of Solomon," shouted the Widow Starr.

"I have put off my coat," said Nocturnal, or maybe it was Propagate, as my mind would oft mix up the two, seeing as they was twins. . . .

Humor is necessary to any good book. To lighten the lyric. For *pace*. But that poses a problem:

What is humor?

I shall give you my definition of the structure of comedy, and let you decide whether or not it makes any sense.

Humor is a bridge, a connection, a sudden span that unites two previously disassociated entities. It is that surprising arc-jump of light that flashes between anode and cathode. Comedy is a marriage of two things, two ideas, two beings that were never before connected.

Neil Simon's right. Humor is *The Odd Couple*.

I like Neil Simon. He puts two chunks of matter

together that don't belong in the same phone booth. And it's funny.

A joke is so often a commonplace situation that progresses into a most unusual end. A twist. A punch line.

I don't know who said this: When I was born, I was so ugly the doctor slapped my mother. Even she hated me. Mother used to park my baby carriage in a tow-away zone.

Comedy is good for us.

Comedians are pleasant fellows. The great names of comedy were and are affable people and not mean or ornery. Jack Benny was a delight. Ditto for Bob Hope, Groucho Marx, Eddie Cantor, Fred Allen and Bob Newhart.

Don't get your laughs at the expense of someone else's pain. And never write a book to get even with an enemy. Laugh with people, not at them.

Laugh at yourself.(Woody Allen does.) Keep a list of all the dumb things you've done in your life and share with your readers just how absurd you are. Take your work seriously instead of yourself.

Knowing what humor is will help you lighten your literature. Add a cello to your tuba.

Get to Know Charlie Hopple

I met Angus on a train.

My briefcase was open, on my knees, and I was busily jotting down scribble after scribble. The gentleman sitting next to me politely asked if I was writing a book. I was.

As it turned out, he worked as an editor at Knopf, and he introduced himself as Angus Cameron. We had lunch. It was then that I asked him what, in his opinion, was the most important thing in a book. Was it plot?

"No," said Angus. "It is *character*."

Little did I know that, years later, Knopf would publish my first novel, *A Day No Pigs Would Die*.

Angus Cameron's advice turned out to be solid.

Let's say you decide to write a book, about a family that owns a modest paper mill and lives in a small town. Okay, you have solved two easy questions, what and where. Now comes the pivotal problem, the most important question that you face prior to starting Chapter 1.

Who?

Who are your characters?

Let's say there are three principal characters, A, B, and C. Whip out a fresh piece of paper and jot down everything you know about A. Let's call him Mr. A.

What does he look like? Fat? Thin? Tall?

How old is he? And how old does he feel?

Is he fifty-five? Getting a little gray, a little bald, a bit paunchy?

Is he a Protestant, a Catholic, a Jew?

Is he liberal or conservative?

Republican or Democrat?

Rural or urban? Is he the one, but wants to be the other?

Is he sick or well? Does he cough? Spit?

Is he single, married, or divorced?

Gay or straight?

Does he collect stamps, or blondes?

Most important: What does he do for a living? What are his dreams? His goals? This will lead you to what Mr. A *wants*. And, if he wants what belongs to someone else, you have yourself a plot.

Does he hate his wife? Fear his boss? Flirt with his secretary?

Is Mr. A allergic? Constipated? Frustrated?

When his car doesn't start, does he beat the steering wheel with his fists?

Does he swear? Does he pray? Does he yell? If so, at whom? Does he ever throw a punch, or a tantrum?

When he works only half a day at the office, does he take off his white shirt at noon and wonder if he can wear it tomorrow?

Does he smell it?

Before you begin Chapter 1, be sure to outline all your characters so that you know them inside and out. This book, you see, is not about making paper. The paper mill town is just scenery, a backdrop. The novel is about Mr. A. He's the one you must originally study and finely draw.

Know . . . your . . . folks.

Because if you know them, they will help you write your book. So get to know them so well that they actually begin to talk to you. To say things. Do things. *Want* things.

Give each character a name.

Who is Mr. A? Let's call him Charlie Hopple.

Where was Charlie born and raised?

What did he do as a kid?

And what are his tastes? Could you see Charlie flip through *TV Guide* and know, as he knows, which show he'll watch? Would he twig to M.A.S.H. and hate Bonanza?

Does he do his own income tax? Does he cheat? Is he proud of it or frightened by it?

At the office, where does Charlie Hopple rank? Is he the boss or the janitor? Are there two bright young men (with MBA degrees from Harvard Business School) rising fast behind him, and does Charlie feel their breath on the back of his neck?

Is he scared?

Is there a real threat to his career, or is Charlie paranoid?

What is Charlie good at? Bowling, or dancing? What situations embarrass him? Know his strong points and his soft spots. Make sure you know what makes him laugh, or cry.

If he had his life to live over, what would he do differently?

What events in his childhood does Charlie Hopple remember? Or try to forget? Was there ever one special toy that he treasured or was it a wished-for toy that he never got to own? Is it a teddy bear? A sled? Rosebud?

When he is at the office, is Charlie Hopple secure enough to answer his own telephone when it rings, or does he ask his secretary to do it? Or does he work in the mill itself? How does Charlie treat people who work under him, as opposed to the people who are above him?

What kind of neckties does he wear? Are his cuffs frayed, his collars?

Does he play poker every Friday night? Is he an Elk, a Rotarian, or a Mason?

Once you get to know Charlie Hopple, you will be able to observe him. You'll hear the rough rasp of his voice; watch him buckle his belt, sign his name, sneeze.

What's his favorite food? Does he have one favorite dish that he insists on preparing all by himself, outlandishly attired in a matching apron and chef's hat?

Now, if you know all this info, you are prepared to start your novel. Charlie will be thinking, talking, and acting so fast that your pen will have to race just to put it all down on paper. That's how character bursts into life.

Most important, I say to you again, is that you discover what Charlie Hopple *wants*. Because that one desire will be the thrust of your novel:

1. Charlie wants something.
2. He tries to get it.
3. He is opposed.

So get to know Charlie Hopple and *he* will do a lot of your work.

Beware of Ludlow Goodpants

Ever heard of Ludlow?

No, you never have. I just invented him. Yet you've read books in which Ludlow Goodpants is the faultless hero. Clean, prissy, and dull. And you've seen him on TV many times.

Ludlow Goodpants is usually played by someone like Arthur Hill. Always a liberal, an intellectual, a goody-goody with a padlock on his inner feelings. What's more, Ludlow will be the first to tell you, just before he bites into his steak, that he's *so* opposed to violence.

Here's a TV example:

Owen Marshall: Counselor at Law.

Owen (Arthur Hill) is nice nice nice. If Mafia hit men were squeezing off a bullet in the back of Owen's head, he wouldn't even say boo. Because, you see, Owen (A.K.A. Ludlow Goodpants) hates John Wayne but absolutely *adores* Jane Fonda.

Where is *Owen* today?

Down the tube. Not on it. *Owen* didn't last very long. Ludlow was just too good to be true.

Compare, if you will please, Ludlow Goodpants to a guy who wasn't so good, or nice.

Archie Bunker.

Good old Arch and that big Irish face became an American folk hero, a champion of the blue collar Joe. Admit it. You loved him, too.

All in the Family, Archie's show, was top-rated in the Nielsen's year after year, season upon season.

Archie was seldom very nice. Arch worked hard, fed his family, kept a roof over their heads. On the other hand, his views were narrow, unfair, bigoted; and his temper often flew out of control. He was real. Like you and me. Sometimes tender and sometimes loud. At other times, Arch could be warm and sensitive.

America was loyal to Mr. Bunker. "Tell 'em, Arch!" Because old Archie spoke for the people, the workers, the folks. Things that bothered him bothered them. And us. Taxes, government, busing . . . and, most of all, *change*. Life was, we all think, better in the Good Old Days.

We look at Archie Bunker and who do we see? Ourselves. He is in all of us just as we all are in him. Archie is humanity. A delightful and hateful blend of fault and folly and fatherhood. He is real.

Let Archie be a lesson to you. If you have a hero in your book, pour two ingredients into your mixing bowl: good and bad. Don't make him another Ludlow Goodpants.

(Here's a twist. Wouldn't you enjoy seeing Owen Marshall playing the part of Archie Bunker?)

So if you have a hero, take the fellow out back and throw him in the swamp. Rub some mud on the guy. Get him dirty. Make him real. How dirty? Well, just make sure that your literary hero is every bit as much of a stinker as *you* are.

Are you always nice nice nice?

If you are, congratulations. Not to be cynical, there's good in all people. Will Rogers (or was it Zsa Zsa Gabor?) always said "I never met a man I didn't like." I think it was *Will* who said it.

Study the character of Skinner Benet in *Eagle Fur*.

Here are two extracts from the book. In the first Abbott Coe, a bonded servant of Benet's, is thinking *and feeling.* In the second Benet is talking to Coe and Ensign McKee, a young soldier, around their campfire.

I laughed. But before my smile was complete, the hand of Skinner Benet whipped from his body, a swift arrow from a ready bow, catching my jaw with force to spin me halfway about. His moc struck in the crotch, from the rear, and I was near to vomiting with pain. Why? The kick hurt so badly that I dared not even turn to face my master to ask what I had done to incite his temper. . . .

What had I done to him? Offended him?

Benet was a coiled snake. The man was a walking keg of powder, black and gritty, abrim with charcoal and sulphur and saltpeter, ready to explode. And no crackling torch of a cannoneer was necessary. Aye, even a spark. A red-hot speck from a flint as futile as mine would ignite old Skinner Benet. Nor could anyone predict how, or where his touch-hole, or why.

"Ensign, would you willfully exchange this solemn mass of solitude for cannon and bagpipe?"

McKee was silent. "At the moment, sir, nay, I should not."

"Would you see these forests nourished by the rotting of wounded Highlanders and Welsh and Irish lads? I will not, McKee. Not to please you or Braddock or King George. Not even for the Hudson's Bay Company. Were there only a way."

"A way to what, sir?"

"Now that we have taken Canada, torn her open, and trapped her treasure, if only we could reseal her again. Roll a mighty stone to mask the mouth of her crypt. If only we'd all leave and allow Canada to rest and lick her wounds, and return ourselves to Europe."

McKee and I were silent.

"At night," said Benet, "I smell the stench of Fort Albany and a garrison latrine, and I hear Canada scream in torment. For to me she is a maiden fair who is being raped and ravaged. Furs torn from her modesty. And somewhere, a litter of beaver kits cry hungrily for a mother who'll not return from iron jaws."

I wanted to say words, but none would come. So I waited for McKee to speak. He, too, kept the silence.

"You see," said Benet softly, "I have no sons."

He stood up. Before he walked off to his blanket, his hand lightly touched our faces. Owen's, then mine.

Is he all good, all evil? Selfish? Giving? A blend? Is he both tender and tinder?

I suppose some people might not agree with me, but were I to choose a friend, I would pick Archie Bunker and not some faultless (and unreal) fellow that exists only in the mind of a television writer.

Stick to Archie. Lovable? Maybe not. But no one can say he ain't a human bean.

Beware of Ludlow Goodpants.

Laurel and Hardy

Remember them?

Back when I was a kid, seeing a Laurel & Hardy movie was the closest I ever got to Heaven.

Two funny men. What made them tops in their field was the fact that their personalities were totally different. They were not Tweedledee and Tweedledum. Stan was little and skinny; Ollie was big and fat. Stan was meek and mild; Ollie was assertive, the boss.

They would not have been interesting had they been two Laurels or two Hardys.

This is a rut into which the emerging writer tends to stumble: He makes his characters too bland, too much alike, so much so that it is difficult to tell them apart, one from another.

Let's examine some pairs of people:
George Burns and Gracie Allen.
Sherlock Holmes and Dr. Watson.
Bud Abbott and Lou Costello.
King Henry and Falstaff.
Mutt and Jeff.
Felix Unger and Oscar Madison.
Mork and Mindy.

Just like Stan Laurel and Oliver Hardy, the above teams

were different as night and day, but somehow paired like ham 'n' eggs.

Sooner or later, almost every neophyte writer says, "I think I'll try to write a book for children. It ought to be a snap."

It isn't.

Editors who specialize in selecting books for young readers are just as fussy as the editors in adult fiction. They, too, want contrast.

I made this mistake once. My two characters were close to being identical twins. They were like Pat and Mike, the tipsy stars of so many boring Irish jokes. Or like Flopsy and Mopsy in *Peter Rabbit*. You couldn't tell which was which.

Finally I wised up, and wrote *Soup*, which is part of the ABC Weekend Special series.

In case you haven't read *Soup* or *Soup and Me* or *Soup for President* or *Soup's Drum*, this series of books features two boys: Rob (me) and my best pal Soup, two kids who live on adjacent farms in Vermont, back in the 1930s.

Rob tells the story in the first person, and the camera is always inside his head. He is the smaller and younger of the two boys; quieter, more cautious, and the reflective philosopher who records the action.

Soup is bigger and is also the protagonist, the troublemaker. He is the brains of the outfit, the Dr. Johnson, while Rob is Soup's shadow, his Boswell.

Soup makes the mischief. Rob is the fall guy—somehow he usually gets blamed for the messes they fall into.

Conversations between the two boys are, therefore, a cinch to write. Because of what's being said, the reader always knows who is talking, without names in every speech.

Better yet, Soup books are fun to write, which (I hope) makes them fun to read. Not just to read for one's own pleasure, but to read aloud to a classroom of kids.

Now, if Soup and Rob were literary twins, much of the magic would be gone.

After graduating from Laurel & Hardy movies, I advanced to a rapt appreciation of two other fellows, Dean Martin and Jerry Lewis.

Their early films were classic comedy.

Yet they, too, would have failed had their personalities been Tweedledee and Tweedledum.

Moving from a duet to a trio, take a stab at reading a historical novel I wrote about the American Revolution, entitled The King's Iron.

There are three principal characters. Mentally draw a circle and a square and a triangle. Or do it on paper. The difference among the geometric shapes is manifested in the leading characters of this novel:

Durable Hatch is a crusty old Vermont woodsman and trapper who takes a bath every July whether he needs it or not.

Cotton Mayfield Witty is a haughty young Virginian, a patrician, a spoiled brat who believes in fast horses and young ladies of equal speed.

Blue Goose is a Huron warrior. He is silent, religious,

reflective, and more loyal to old Hatch than Tonto was to the Lone Ranger. And he is also an absolute savage.

Here are some examples of each character's thoughts. Even without the names you would know at a glance that we have three very different folks here.

Durable Hatch ignored the request. Damn that young cur and his infernal horses. Let his legs ache as my back still aches from the pounding I took astride that cussed animal. Devil take him. *His* turn to follow, by dang, and follow he will; as it sure ain't my intending to ease up on him. Trot, you young buck. Trot until you puke up your breakfast all over the Dutch woods, and neither Blue Goose nor me'll as much as wipe your chin. So work them kiddy legs off, on account you don't keep stride with me and Blue, you are one lost babe.

Turning his head and his thoughts, Cotton Witty watched the old man and the Huron trying to mount their horses. Worst two plugs I could find, he snickered to himself. A mare and a gelding, neither at home under a saddle or under a man's weight. Suddenly the black mare whipped around her head, her lips curled, as her yellow teeth found the bony shoulder of Durable Hatch. Shaking her head, she shook the old trapper as a dog shakes a snake. Witty smiled. To add to the merriment, the gelding kicked the red man, sending him sprawling into a stack of newly-made kegs. The small barrels tumbled down upon the poor savage as though he'd shaken a tree of ripe pears.

I wonder, thought Blue Goose, if my white man grows ill with worry for his red friend. Were I in the canoe and he up here, my hands would be wet for his safety. Does he pray? He does not speak of his God to me and yet I know that he has one for he says "God!" when he drops his food into the fire, and repeats the name when his hand burns in trying to retrieve it. Yes, my white man must have a God to worship. I believe all men do, be they of red skin or of white. How could a man think not of a God, unless he has never seen the night sky dusted with stars?

Three is a good number to work with. Why do you think they call it the *eternal* triangle?

If two children are happily playing together, what happens when a third child joins the scene? Chaos. You can't be either a parent or a kid and not have learned this.

Three means trouble.

Have you ever seen *The Three Stooges*?

Curly and Larry and Moe were alike, yet different. At least visually. Remembering them brings to mind another great trio: Groucho, Chico, and Harpo . . . the Marx Brothers.

They were far more successful than the Stooges, because of their depth of individual comic characterization. Groucho was the acid-witted plotter, Harpo the lovable and silent clown, Chico the Italian-accented piano player with hands like flippers.

Beauty is variety. That's how a pro creates.

Bless you, Stan and Ollie.

Hamlet and a Casting Couch

I once saw a play called *Hamlet*.

Once. It was so long and drawn out that I would never force myself to sit through it again. I suppose the play is considered by scholars to be a classic. The playwright's name escapes me.

You know what a classic is. It's the kind of a book that teachers *make* you read.

In case you missed *Hamlet* when it was in town (because you went to see Burt Reynolds), there's a character in the play named Polonius, a gossipy old busybody who is shipping his kid, Laertes, off to either school or summer camp.

Polonius lays on Laertes a few trite tidbits of advice, so that he doesn't hang out with the wrong crowd, or get busted:

"Neither a borrower nor a lender be."

Good advice?

Maybe, but not for a writer.

Everybody swipes. Think about your expense account or your income tax return. Is there any greater joy than ripping up a speeding ticket? Or stealing a cookie?

Artists are borrowers.

Ever been to an art show? Who do you see there,

strolling around in the sunshine, looking at all the paintings and sketches and ceramic whales? I'll tell you who. Artists.

Are they thieves? No, not at all. But all artists borrow from the style and technique of other artists. One artist looks at a burlap zebra framed in wormy driftwood and says . . .

"I bet *I* could do that. And do it better."

Sure you can.

Read a lot of stuff. Browse in bookstores. See what's being done, sold, and then go do it yourself. Why should *you* starve?

Bob Hope wrote a book in which he claimed that all of his original jokes had been later "tested and approved by Milton Berle."

Uncle Milty even said, in a TV commercial, "I know a joke when I steal one."

When I was named director of the Rollins College Writers Conference, one of the speakers I invited was a Rollins prof, a man who had taught me when I was a student there. His name is Wilbur Dorsett.

He's a nifty gent. And brilliant.

On stage, he ended his presentation by reading the

closing passages of John Steinbeck's *Of Mice and Men*. It is a story of two men, George and Lenny, who have formed a friendship for their mutual protection and survival. George is a small man with brains. Lenny is a simpleminded but gentle giant who protects George with muscle.

At the book's end, Lenny inadvertently kills someone. And then George shoots and kills Lenny to prevent the authorities from locking up poor Lenny like an animal. The book is a tragedy about having to destroy that one person you most dearly care for.

Wilbur Dorsett's reading made me cry.

Afterward, I began to wonder if a book about such a friendship (between a normal mind and a retarded one) could be written for children.

So I wrote *Clunie.*

Even though my book about a young girl named Clunie Finn has nothing directly to do with *Of Mice and Men*, I hope that John Steinbeck will forgive my borrowing.

Movie stars lend things to me for just about every book I write. So here's a tool that I have found to be quite useful. A tool that I shall, in turn, gladly lend to your toolkit:

Hold a casting session.

Before starting the first chapter of your novel, let's say that you decide on three major characters:

Clemson Grange, the father.

Andy, his son.

Pamela, the father's girlfriend.

Now ask yourself this: If a movie based on your book were to be shot, *whom* would you cast in these three roles?

Is your father a Gregory Peck, a Henry Fonda, a Fred MacMurray? Is the son a Woody Allen or a Robert Redford?

And is the girlfriend, Pamela, a Julie Christie or a Julie Newmar?

Do this, and something magical will happen. You will start to see and hear Gregory Peck as your fictional father. His phrasing and mannerisms will impart a new depth and dimension to Clemson Grange's character. He'll have a face and a voice. A body, a certain walk. Yet it won't be Gregory Peck. It'll flesh out into a real Clemson Grange.

I do this, and it works like a charm.

You'll be amazed as to how much Gregory Peck will add to Mr. Grange's personality and attitude. You may even stay up until three o'clock in the morning, watching the late show, just to see Gregory Peck as the father, Atticus Finch, in *To Kill a Mockingbird*.

And, near the close of that motion picture, when the dignified old black grandfather says to Mr. Finch's two children . . . "Stand up. Your father is passing by . . . " if you don't cry, then I guess I have little hope for your heart or your pen.

So, in conclusion, curl up on your casting couch with Julie Newmar and see if the couch fits Julie's long legs . . . and if Julie fits Pamela's pantyhose.

Thus you'll discover if a combination of Julie and Gregory and Woody Allen all add up to *Hamlet*.

Borrow.

John and Marsha

Do you remember Stan Freberg?

A generation ago, he produced a comic record, comprising two voices, one male and one female. Their names were John and Marsha. For the entire side, all Marsha said was "John" and all John said was "Marsha." The two grew emotionally involved and the panting conclusion was a howl.

Now that you remember John and Marsha, it's high time you forgot them. Forever.

Emerging writers do this too much:

"Hello, John."

"Hi there, Marsha."

"Nice party we're at, John."

"Love your dress, Marsha. New?"

"John, it's just an old rag."

"Wanna dance, Marsha?"

"Love to, John."

"You sure sweat a lot, Marsha."

"Do I, John?"

"Worse'n our mule, Marsha."

"You have a mule named Marsha, John?"

"Yes, Marsha. John's our boarhog."

"A boarhog named John, John?"
"Yup. And a mule called Marsha, Marsha."

A style like this makes me wonder how such writers would handle a conversation between two men, both of whom were named Harold.

I think I know why emerging writers do this. They want their readers to know who is speaking. But if the reader can't tell who is talking, then the characters and their personalities are ill-defined.

Here's another booby trap:

Amateurs worry about overusing the word *said* when two characters converse, so much so that they herd in every substitute for *said* they can muster.

"Hello," said George.
"Hi," Janet whispered.
"Busy tonight?" asked George.
"No," replied Janet.
"How about a date?" George inquired.
"Thought you'd never ask," Janet responded.
"Wear something slinky," George suggested.
"My filmy black nightie," Janet panted.

"Yes!" George ejaculated.

Worse than that (if anything could be) the amateur seems compelled to describe *how* the obvious was stated . . . by adding useless *ly* adverbs following each *said*.

"Here come ten thousand Sioux," said Custer excitedly.
"And thank the goodness," George said eagerly, "they're all girls."
"In filmy black nighties," said Custer amazedly.
"But I don't see Janet," said George apprehensively.
"Third nightie from the left," Custer said knowingly.

In music, between phrases of melody, you play what is known as a passing chord, a filler. In writing, that's what *said* is. Don't be afraid that you've said *said* too often. Nobody reads it. The eye skips over it. In a sentence like " 'Here come the Sioux,' said Custer," no eye is going to rest on *said* very long. There just isn't time.

While I'm at it, I might as well repeat a few hints that my editors at Doubleday, Knopf, and Little, Brown have passed along to me.

Avoid exclamation marks!!!

Amateurs bang one in at darn near the end of every sentence! Don't do it! Stop! Please!

And while you're at it, quit underlining every other word because you think it's important. Until you drive a Lincoln, nothing you say or think or do is important.

One more thing. You can "jolly well quick" stop using pair after pair of what might be called these "Billy be damned" quotation marks that you want to use "until Hell freezes over" in your narrative; because if you can "kick the habit," your style will improve and may even "pull itself up by its bootstraps."

Examine my novels.

You'll really have to hunt, search, and turn over rocks before you find your first (my first) exclamation mark!

But you'll also see that I've said *said* a thousand times.

Repetition (other than *said*) is, however, boring, boring, boring. So my advice to you is to avoid it as much as possible. Your cowboy character's gun can also be his pistol, or his weapon, or his .45. If you've written *horse* three times in one paragraph, slip in a *steed*, or a *mount*; or refer to it as an *animal*.

Getting back to John and Marsha (even though I told you please, once and for always, to forget about them two), writing good dialogue is tough, and we'll handle that one later in the book.

By the way, I lied to you earlier. John doesn't have a mule named Marsha. I made it all up.

Meanwhile, next time you engage in a conversation, or overhear one, notice:

When a person talks to another person, he hardly ever speaks the name of the other person. Perhaps at the opening of the chat. . ."Hi, Babs." and at their parting . . . "So long, Babs." But rarely during.

So, you can finally forget John and Marsha.

Unless you get your kicks remembering mules and boarhogs.

Give Me a Hand

My mother died in October of 1976.

Whenever I picture her in my mind, I so often see her hands. She had the hands of a Vermont farmwife: hard and lean and twisted with work.

Her hands were capable and caring, as her fingers patched up worn overalls that she had scrubbed to near white. The original blue, as well as day after day's dirt, had been washed and rinsed away. I often wondered how those hands that tackled so much soil could always be so clean.

Emerging writers usually tell me what color a character's hair is. Or eyes. Compared to a hand, eyes and hair are ho-hum. Give me a good old hand any day. Because, by comparison, a hand does so much work and bestows so much more care and comfort.

Oddly enough, the first syllable in the word character is *care*.

As soon as you make your character care for someone, or something (even an old pipe), the reader begins to care about what happens to the character. But the care must be for something or someone other than himself.

Here's an example:

13.

Bowing our heads to give thanks, I heard Papa say the blessing at our supper table. As I always did, I peeked up just once to see his hands. Noah Booker had big hands, and when he offered up his gratefulness at mealtime, he locked his hands together, in prayer. His fingers were thick with work, and the way he held them reminded me of the rafters of a church. Whenever he spoke our blessing, he pressed his thumbs against the brow of his bowed head, and then he sort of built a church with his hands.

Hands *do.*

A mouth can merely say "I care," yet a mother's or father's hand can tuck a winter quilt up under a child's chin.

Hands perform. It is easy for a writer to describe what job a hand is doing. But, to digress for a paragraph or two, it is much more difficult for a writer to picture *language.*

Yet it can be done.

I am Mohawk, said his heart. Growing up, Fawn

had talked much to his grandfather, Old Foot, and it was soft as his mother's singing. They spoke as the wind to leaves, as the brook to pebbles. Mohawk words were happy words that fly from the mouth like tiny wrens.

Above, I was writing about sound; yet the sound is shown by a series of pictures . . . of leaves, pebbles, wrens.

Again, there is no need for the author to hit the reader over the head and proclaim that Fawn loves Old Foot. Or earlier in this chapter, that young Able Booker (sitting at his supper table) respects his father, Noah.

The reader understands.

Hands are most useful in writing because a hand usually brings action, as opposed to just thoughts and conversation. It is near impossible to write a novel about human beings and not have a hand darn a sock or pull a trigger or *do* something. The infinite versatility of the human hand, constantly in motion, so often keeps a story churning. Each time somebody does something, a hand is involved.

You can *talk* about *kindness* until your reader is hopelessly bored. But his interest perks up as soon as a hand pets a kitten. Or cocks a rifle.

Speaking of boredom, I have no doubt bored you by continually begging you to make a picture. I bore you so *you* don't bore your readers with pictureless prose.

Hands make nifty pictures.

When a hand on a dark street suddenly clicks open a switchblade knife, your reader does not lay down the book.

Please don't get the idea that I'm promoting violence as the chief tool to interest a reader. No way. Yet we all do live in a violent world. Luckily it is also a world rife with tenderness.

Learn to describe, in your work, how a hand speaks love, and your style will brighten.

Example:

A little girl and her father have popped some popcorn. The bowl from which they eat is abrim with white fluffy kernels that are soon nibbled and swallowed. Only a few kernels remain in the bottom of the bowl. Some are white and fluffy, others black and hard. The little girl's hand reaches for the black kernels, leaving the white popcorn for her father.

Hands talk, and express so much feeling.

Our hands make music as well as mayhem and murder. And, somewhere in between, young hands get into many a merry mischief which is sometimes neither good nor bad. Just childlike.

Hands help and hands hinder.

A hand is sometimes the very soul of a helpmate, as on a farm where you have a family plus a *hired hand*. Caution: Beware of "the toilworn fingers of Mother Machree." Don't slop too much syrup on those dear old fingers. If in doubt, don't overwrite. Underwrite.

· And, to describe (picture) a character in your novel, please don't tell me much about the color of hair and eyes. That's just a cosmetic ad. Instead, show somebody helping someone else to *do* a chore; fight somebody; fix something; heal somebody.

Give me a hand.

Sound Reasoning

I love SFX.

One evening at a cocktail party I overheard a writer (who had published nothing) make the comment "For a novel to sell today, it has to have plenty of SEX."

I don't agree. What it does have to have is SFX.

What is SFX?

I'll tell you . . . as you are, I presume, old enough to know.

When you write a script for a radio (or television) commercial, and you need to establish for the listener (or viewer) that it is morning on a farm, you jot down something like this:

SFX: ROOSTER CROW.

SFX means *sound effects*.

Crisp fiction, like a refreshing radio or TV spot, has to emit sound: the *plump* of a pebble that is tossed into a pond. If Roland is your character, let the reader hear what Roland hears. (The softly retreating beats of Muriel's heart?)

Make sure that your readers hear what Roland is hearing. If he's human, he's *got* to be surrounded by some sort of racket.

Are there SFX in bed?

If so, bless my ear with the twang of Muriel's mattress, or the creak of her bedpost, or the drip of a faucet. Muriel's nocturne has some sort of a hubbub, even if it's only a few sawing snores from Roland!

Sound is one of the spices of fiction, to perk a reader's ear (and eye) and make him feel he's really there.

I used SFX in the third chapter of *Fawn*.

The boy has slept alone on a quiet island in Lake George, in the year 1758; he awakens to hear the distant, slowly approaching, bagpipes of the advancing soldiers. Fawn Charbon has never before heard a bagpipe.

Later in the novel a young French sentry, standing watch at dawn on the battlements of Fort Ticonderoga, hears those same bagpipes.

Speaking of the sounds of war, before writing *Fawn*, and needing to know exactly what an arrow in flight sounds like, I asked a friend of mine, a bow hunter, to shoot one at me. I ordered him to miss my ear by only a few inches. Not wanting (coward that I am) to re-enact the role of William Tell's little boy, I hid behind a tree and *listened*.

It went whipping by my ear with a very definite SFX. The arrow *hissed!*

For a novel entitled *Justice Lion*, I created a character whose name is Rake Tatum. He is a lawman, a country sheriff in a small Vermont town, who walks with a limp and a cane. One foot drags as he hobbles along, scratching the sidewalk with every other step. No reader will remember how Rake Tatum *looks* as he walks, but they will remember how Rake *sounds*.

As he approaches, you (the reader) will *hear* Rake coming down the street. The noise of his walk is a part of the characterization.

Justice Lion is a courtroom novel, about a trial; Judge Henry Gleason's gavel raps often to punctuate the courtroom procedure, in counterpoint to the constant rumbles of audience reaction.

Earlier in the book, Chapter 1 begins with an auditory adventure. It opens with a sound:

Two boys, Muncie Bolt and Hem Lion, are lying on their backs on a bed of pine needles in moonlight, listening to the bugling of a pair of Hem's hounds that are chasing a coon. Hem is a mountain boy whose ear can read every bark, Muncie is a town boy who's a tad confused.

Practice SFX at home.

Right now, is there someone in your kitchen preparing a meal? Close your eyes and picture the action amid the clatter of pots and pans and crockery, the jingle of silverware, and the gurgle of tap water filling a tumbler; illustrate in your mind's eye exactly what you hear.

Listen to a man shoeing a horse.

Stop off at a construction site, and close your eyes to paint the whang-bang action by sound. Try not to feel what your dentist is doing but rather hearken to the taps, scrapes, and whirrs of his instruments.

Ask yourself, What are the noises of evening as opposed to those of morning?

Pretend you are blind and you are waking up early in

the morning on a farm in the 1930s. Does a farmer cough? Pull on heavy work boots? Does he clump down the stairs to slam a kitchen door? Open up a barn? Listen to the clank of a pair of metal milk pails and the soft, ponderous, breathing of a Holstein? Can you hear the farmer's hand gently pat her, crowd her away from the wall; hear his voice, still foggy with sleep, speak to her as their day begins together?

He wipes the grit from her udder, sets a pail beneath her . . . then the straight streams of milk begin to chime into his pail. It is a steady pulse of milk, and work, and of a living moment of morning on a farm.

Can you hear other chores? A rustle of hay tumbling into a manger? Wooden bars thrust aside to turn the cows out into a meadow where larks are nesting?

Who else comes to the barn? A little laughing girl? A barn cat who mews for her morning spray of milk? Is she purring?

Are there bleating goats? Sheep? Lambs? A hungry calf? Can you hear a tractor start? A shovel biting into earth or the silver of a plowshare swimming its furrow?

Does a schoolbus stop, honk, pull away?

As the farmer drops a leather harness to the broad back of a Percheron, hear the traces buckle and snap, and the horse snort. Listen to the drumming of a heavy hoof as the big horse raps his iron to a barn's wooden floor. There is no sound to equal it; it is the beating of the drum of my long-ago home. An echo of my memories.

Now do the same thing with an experience (or memory) from *your* life. Exercise your ears.

Maybe you've been so busy talking that you've never quite bothered to *hear* anything.

Yet your reader wants to hear. Hum him a tune. Strum a ukulele. Stick a bee in his bonnet. Or a jackhammer! Is the kid next door practicing her trombone, and are her parents having a spat over it? Will someone throw a saucepan? If the pan Muriel throws misses Roland, does it shatter a window—tinkle the glass? Through that busted pane you should be able to hear Roland swear.

Give your character an earache; and then let your reader *hear* it, as well as feel it.

Good fiction has SFX appeal.

Rug a Reader

Y ou're throwing a bash.

It's March, and mud abounds. So you place a mat (a foot rug) outside your front door upon which your guests may wipe their feet. One word is printed on the mat in big letters:

SCRAM.

Of course you wouldn't do this for the opening of your party. Yet so many emerging writers do it when they open a chapter. They begin chapters with big paragraphs, giant blocks of copy that say SCRAM instead of WELCOME.

Let's picture a reader.

Her name is Rose Tarzanski, and she's worked all day at the check-out counter of a supermarket. Her feet ache. It's late. Her husband, Bruno, had a full day at Midas Muffler and hit the sack an hour ago.

Rose is lying on her living room sofa, shoes off, hair in curlers, reading your book. As the clock bongs midnight, she finishes Chapter 6.

Does she close the book?

Not quite yet. Her eyes flick to the first line of Chapter 7. If it's a big paragraph of descriptive narrative, Rose

shuts the book. But, if Rose sees "Drop that gun," you've got her hog-tied.

A short and snappy chapter opening like that will win Rose every time. She'll stay up until two a.m., and complain the next day that she "just couldn't put that book down."

So my advice to you is, hook Rose Tarzanski with the opening of each chapter. Grab her, ruin her night's rest, and let Bruno cook his own breakfast.

Put out your welcome mat. Rug her!

Do I do it? Open any of my novels to any chapter and examine my chapter openings. Usually my first paragraph is composed not only of one line, but of very few words. Often my first paragraph is less than half a line long. And that paragraph is always physical and immediate. Someone is talking about something important, which pulls the reader right into the book. Here are a few examples:

From *The King's Iron*:

> "General Washington will see you, sir."
>
> I hurt, thought Blue Goose.

"He is dead, sir."

Will I ever again walk?

From *Fawn*:

The rum was gone.

A page in a novel is not a block of text. Readers hate this, and have since childhood, because it reminds them of textbooks.

Think back to when you were a kid, and you were ordered by your teacher to trudge down to the library and select a book to read. What did you do? You did what I did. You flipped through a book to find pages that were riddled with white space, short paragraphs, and fast-moving palaver:

"Marsha?"

"Is that you, John?"

"Yes, I'm outside. Beneath your window."

"Can't you find the ladder?"

"No."

"Father's hidden it again."

"Last week he removed all the rungs."

"Climb up the vine, John."

"Here I come."

"Hurry, John. I can't wait."

"Then climb halfway down to meet me."

"I'm climbing. I'm climbing!"

"Marsha, you're in my arms once more."

"What rough arms you have, darling."

"That's the vine, Marsha."

If you yen to be an author, learn to open up your pages to welcome a reader's eye. A book page must not only read well, it must also *look inviting*. Open, like a panoramic painting. Not a close-up of a prison wall, which is how a page appears to a reader if it happens to be a wall of words. An artistic page in a novel has white space aplenty.

An author is an artist.

Paint your page with generous hunks of nothing. Examine a page of any of my many novels and you'll see how open it looks. So don't fence your reader in, or push Rose away. She deserves a WELCOME, not a SCRAM.

Please remember that the welcome that you, the author, offer Rose, the reader, is more than just a snappy chapter opening. The *whole page* must entice, attract, and woo.

Your page is your party. Be inviting.

At your dinner party, would you seat a dozen of your guests around a card table? Emerging writers do. They cram and jam a page with prodigious paragraphy that says SCRAM to poor Rose and her tired eyes.

Invite her, welcome her eye to an open vista instead of pushing her face against a wall of words. Your reader is your friend, your guest. Rose joined Book of the Month Club, or Literary Guild, and shelled out ten bucks to come to your party.

Rug her.

Poetry and Pushups

Why do people do push-ups?

To get stronger, to build muscle, to keep in shape; and to look good in a swimsuit. To impress Mildred.

Push-ups and poems have plenty in common. So I suggest that aspiring fiction writers write a poem every day.

Why?

To get rich? No. Chances are your poems won't be published. Even if they are, the price of poetry is so low that you'll just about pay for your pen and paper.

But poetry builds the muscle of prose.

Every poem, like every push-up, helps you to flex you fiction. As prose is a work of art, a poetic style helps make your art artful. Poetry adds a professional gloss to your words. It buffs a shine on your boot.

So many people think that poetry has to be about agony, heartbreak, searching, experience, Life. No, it does not. Good poetry, like good prose, is based on pictures, tangibility, things, moving parts. Poetry *also* will add cadence (beat, throb, pulse) to your prose.

Start with an object.

Let's say that your grandfather is dead, but you find an old pipe he used to smoke. Show your reader what the

pipe looks like, how it smelled when Gramps smoked it, and how the old gentleman used to hold it in his hand or clench it in his teeth. Did he gesture with it? Talk to it? Strike match after match to keep it lit? Did he knock the ashes out by banging it on the side of his shoe?

Perhaps you might show how your grandfather used the pipe whenever he told you a story about his boyhood.

Did he ever lose the pipe, or misplace it, and then find it again in his pocket?

Was that very pipe a helpmate when he did his work; and if so, what kind of work did he do?

Warning: You don't have to tell your readers that you loved the old gent or that you miss him. This sentiment you can show, if you hold his pipe in *your* hand, holding it just the way you had so often seen the pipe held in *his* hand.

Keep your poetry physical.

Did your grandfather touch you or tickle you? Did you sit on his lap? If so, describe how rough his old trousers were, yet how comforting.

Zero in.

Avoid the painful pitfall of telling too much in a cursory fashion. Instead, tell about one particular time, one moment that you and Gramps shared, one event. The time he yanked a thorn from your toe. Try to write the poem and not use the word *love*.

In the life of every writer there is an old man or an old woman to be cherished and remembered. And if you read my book of poems called *Bee Tree* you'll read about the old folks I remember. And I doubt that you'll read the word *love* in any of the poems. Because *love* is just too precious to be only a four-letter word.

Love is a picture. A touch. One pat on the head or a pinch on a freckled cheek. It is an overt act, a physical exchange between two people, both given and received.

Now then, as there are so many forms of poetry, which one should you try?

A sonnet.

In case you don't know what a sonnet is, it is a poem of fourteen lines, written in iambic pentameter. "One *day*/I *took*/a *walk*/*into*/the *wood*." That is one line of iambic pentameter. Note the five beats (and five offbeats) to a line. A sonnet is three quatraines (three stanzas of four lines each) plus a final rhyming couplet.

This is one of my sonnets, from my book of poems, *Bee Tree*, that was published by Walker and Company:

Cat and Mouse

It is the law. Our cat has caught a mouse.
Across the field she trots with squealing booty.
She'll bring him up the walk, and to the house,
To show us, I suspect, she does her duty.

Lightly in her mouth she holds his head.
A mouse near death, and with a pounding heart.
He knows his time has come. He'll soon be dead.
A warm gray body will be torn apart.

I could scold her for her hunting act,
And take away the mouse that she has caught,
To set him free again in distant tract,
And feed her from a can of food I bought.

I will not disobey the law. I learn
How wrong it is to take what others earn.

Why write sonnets?

Because the sonnet is so rigid in structure that such discipline will drill you closer and closer to perfection of style. Boring and drilling are rather close in meaning; but to write a poem, a good one, is anything but dull.

Dullness comes when the poet refuses to picture his poem.

Words like *love*, *dream*, *agony*, *pain*, and *remembering* have no picture. I, your reader, can't see them. Yet I can see a pipe.

Show me something.

Give it a color, a shape, a smell.

By this, do I mean a flower? Not at all. You can write poetry about things that are less than pleasant, not just about birds and bees and blooms.

Do this often enough and your prose will become poetic, even though the subject on which you write is as unsavory as soiled underwear. To wit . . .

It was late. The bunkhouse was dark, and so I felt my way along a row of snoring men, looking for an empty cot. At first I thought it was occupied, because some lumberjack had hung his long woolen underwear over the high footboard to dry. His underwear suit was soaking wet and it didn't smell too clean. It just hung there, arms down one side and legs down the other, as tired as the man who had soaped it.

Notice, if you would please, the picture in the final sentence.

The writer (me) could have merely said *washed it*. Instead, he wrote *soaped it*, which is sharper. I see a big tired hand holding a brown bar of laundry soap, and he actually scrubs. I see white lather foaming on the gray wool.

I smell the dirty and smell the clean. And I also hear the soap scrubbing, and snores, sounds that whisper the end of a workday.

I believe that there is much poetry in hard work, and that perhaps makes labor an easier topic than love. Work is physical.

Just like poems and push-ups.

Bruce Catton at Bull Run

Thank goodness for Bruce Catton.

Because without Bruce, we never would have been able to enjoy the Civil War. As you know, there never really *was* a war in 1860 or so. Bruce dreamed up the whole shebang, with a little assistance from Margaret Mitchell.

Somebody asked me, "Rob, how come you write so much about history?"

Because there's so much of it.

Look around at the covers of books in a bookstore and what do you so frequently see? People in the garb of yesteryear. In fact, in just about every bookstore there is an entire section stocked with historical novels, Gothic or otherwise.

Isn't it a cheery note to hear that there is far more history than there are writers to write about it? What happened way back in 1979 is history. As to fictional (or film) fads, seems like each new decade nowadays discovers some earlier decade to write about, to dust off and cash in on.

I don't compete with Mr. Catton. My decades are 1750 and 1770, the French and Indian War and the American Revolution.

17.

Neither one of us owns a war. Nobody does. They're all yours to grab and gussy up.

Does an author have to do a lot of research to write a good historical novel? No, not nearly as much as you fear. A few days in a library will let you bone up as much as necessary. After all, a writer of historical novels is not a historian. He's an author. Yet he must be accurate as to who was where when. Build your book on a firm foundation of historical data.

How do you write a historical novel?

Well, here's what I do. And you can do it, too. Just for fun, let's say that you want to do it, and here's how:

Pick one event in history that perks your interest. For example, Washington crossing the Delaware.

Now then, every reader already *knows* that George Washington was on the Pennsylvania shore, crossed in a boat, and landed in Trenton, New Jersey. This is not a wire-hot flash. Allow me to advise you not to begin you book anywhere near the Delaware River. Or, for that matter, even in New Jersey.

Where do you start? Mount Vernon? No. I wouldn't. The first thing you do is close your eyes and picture that dramatic painting of General Washington crossing the

Delaware. He stands bravely at the prow, chin cutting the wind, cape aflow.

Now, with your eyes still shut, conjure up the other occupants of that boat. Hey! See that kid, just behind General Washington, pulling an oar?

Who is he? Is he only seventeen? And what is his name and where did his young life unfold? Where's his home?

To me, a good historical novel is one that shows one event and the people who were there at the time, through the eyes of a fictional character . . . some little nobody corporal.

The kid rowing.

Okay, now we fill in the blanks.

His name is Israel Stoddard, and your novel begins on the Stoddard family farm, in Pennsylvania. The boy's father, William Stoddard, was born in England. Even though he shipped himself and his family to America, William is still loyal to the English crown, and will ever love his sweet England.

His son, Israel, has no memory of England. He crossed the Atlantic in a cradle, at age one. His home is a Pennsylvania farm, with a family he loves, and a chestnut mare he adores.

In your first chapter, perhaps, the Stoddard's mare has been long settled and is about to drop her foal.

If it's a colt, he'll be sold. But, says the father, if it be a filly, then young Israel may keep her and raise her up as his own.

Hot damn! It's a filly. After a few feeble attempts, she wobbles up on her long legs. Israel wipes her dry. Her eyes, wide and searching, see young Israel Stoddard even before they see the mare who bore her.

Her rough tongue gives his face a lick, and he names her: Charity.

Israel hears the neighbors talk about liberty and war.

His father is a Tory, but the boy is a patriot. He enlists in the Continental Army.

On his first night away from home, someone steals his blanket and he sleeps cold. And tries not to cry. He writes home, each of his letters packed with advice on how to groom Charity.

The army is wet, cold, hungry. And still Israel's musket has not yet spat blood. He is a virgin soldier, untried, unbloodied and unbearded. A buttermilk face protrudes from a uniform he swells his chest to fill.

He wrestles with another soldier who took his plate of cold beans and he is beaten.

And the boy is flogged, by his sergeant, for brawling.

Israel meets Papa Sam, an elderly soldier who becomes father and mother to the lad, steadying his musket and helping him to hammer straight a crooked bayonet.

And he meets Sam's granddaughter, Benevolence, who comes with her parents to visit the camp.

By the time the army reaches the snowy banks of the Delaware River, in Chapter 18, your reader is not concerned about whether or not Washington and his troops will cross. Your reader is fretting about what is going to happen to Israel Stoddard and his ladylove; and wondering if the lad will ever return to that farm, and to Charity.

You see, your novel really isn't about crossing the Delaware. *It's about people.* The Delaware is just scenery. And we see Washington only as he is seen through the eyes of Israel Stoddard.

Well, that's one way to do it. It's the way I work. The structure is pig simple. A big event recorded by a little soldier.

So it is no longer your story, or mine, or Bruce Catton's.

It is Israel's.

Titles and Thumbtacks

It was a hot evening.

You drank a gallon or two of iced tea, polished off a quart of lemonade, plus a tall tumbler of milk. Then three bottles of root beer. And went to bed.

Do you ever have to get up in the middle of the night and go somewhere?

There you are in the bedroom, stumbling around in the dark, on your way to the john. Suddenly you discover something. Not at all what you were looking for. In your foot there's a thumbtack.

Ouch.

No one needs to tell you where it's at. You know. That cussed tack is smack-dab in the center of your right heel, and it hurts like holy Hannah.

Titles are like that.

They don't get brainstormed by authors. They just happen. And when you accidentally discover one, you know it for what it is, like an unsuspected tack in the dark.

Titles are darn important.

Here's why: For every one person that reads your current novel, there will be a thousand who will just read your title. And (you hope) remember it. And maybe even

say, "Yes, I've heard of that book." This will boost your sales.

Titles, like you and me, are born.

When I was a little kid on a Vermont farm, there was a fellow named Tom who lived uproad from us. One day he whoa'd his wagon out front, on the dirt road, and my father, Haven Peck, walked out to chat.

The two men were standing there, swapping lies, while I stood at Papa's knee to listen.

"Tom, how many kids ya got now?"

"Got me two. A boy and a girl."

My father, a man who could neither read nor write, smiled. "You're lucky," he said. "A boy and a girl is a king's order."

I'm a man now. And the father of a boy and a girl, Christopher and Anne. Someday, perhaps after they grow up and move off, I'll attempt a book about this little prince and princess who so often make me feel like a king.

I know what my title shall be.

A King's Order.

When I wrote my first book I had no title for it, until I was writing the very last chapter. Looking down at my paper I saw the last six words I had written: A day no pigs would die. Lo! I had suddenly stomped on a thumbtack. *A Day No Pigs Would Die* was a title born.

Years ago, I was a high school dropout. I was sick of plowing and breathing mule gas, so I ran off with a buddy of mine, Tony Reali, and joined the US Army.

It was near the end of World War II, and Tony was frowning because the pair of us might miss the whole show. He said "Rob, let's go hunt Japs."

I pardoned his contraction and we joined up. Both of us were seventeen and considered ourselves to be immortal.

In basic training, down in Alabama's fun-packed Fort McClellan, a third seventeen-year-old joined us. We called ourselves The Big Three. Our new member was a kid from the Bronx, wherever that was. His name was Elliot Lefkowitz. Among the three of us were almost a dozen whiskers.

I'm a Protestant. Reali was sort of a Catholic and Elliot was a Jew. We three almost made poor old Sergeant Maliniak go over the hill. To him, we were not The Big Three. Our sergeant had another name for us.

My Three Tourists.

Whenever there was a dirty detail to do, Sergeant Maliniak yelled out, "I needs three volunteers . . . Lefkowitz, Reali, and Peck."

To us, our old sergeant was mother, father, dog, cat, and grandparent. I think he secretly liked us, but he sure kept this sentiment tightly reined.

Reali and I were leaner than dryspell beans, but Lefkowitz was chubby. He said his mother had always urged him to clean his plate: "Eat, Elliot, eat." Elliot ate. Everything in sight. As a kid he probably even ate his Tonka trucks.

Tony Reali and I somehow got Elliot through basic.

Between us, we dragged him over walls, under barbed wire, and through the delights of Alabama red clay. We even calmed him down the day he crawled up face to face with his first scorpion. I don't guess they have those in the Bronx.

We shipped overseas, to Italy.

Packages of food arrived each week for Elliot, mailed by his mother. By the time all that Kosher salami caught up to the 88th Infantry Division, it smelled ripe enough to float a horseshoe. Unfit for human consumption.

We fed it to Sergeant Maliniak.

That was the day *the jeep* rumbled into our area. Out climbed a guy who must have been six and a half feet tall, had a crowbar for a spine, and a neat little row of stars on the front of his helmet.

He was General Mark Clark.

And he marched right up and talked to us. To *us*, the three little nobodies from nowhere. Asked us where home was, whacked us on the shoulder, and told us he was proud to have us in the Fifth Army. I'll never wash my shoulder. Never.

An old bird-colonel was reviewing troops with him, and as the two men limped off, I heard the old colonel say, "General, were we ever that young?" And the general answered him with just three words:

"Toys of war."

Someday I'm going to write my war novel, about my war. Featuring those three mighty warriors . . . Lefkowitz, Reali, and Peck. But it isn't going to be about Europe, or Italy, or about our division. It's going to be about three kids and a small hunk of Italian dirt, our own little half-acre of Hell.

It won't be a very important book, because I don't suppose we did very important deeds. We came home. I didn't bring back a Nazi flag or a Purple Heart or even VD. But I brought home a *title* that I, for one, will always remember.

It'll be the title of my book.

Toys of War.

Where Were You When the Page Was Blank?

Editors are like pets. Almost human.

At present, I have principally three editors: at Knopf, Doubleday, and Little, Brown. They are wonderful people. I love them, and feed them table scraps.

Yet I am very firm with my editors, and sometimes even frown a bit as I bow to kiss their hands. This is the very least I can do for the folks who prod me into prosperity.

However, according to a soldier named Joyce Kilmer, only God can make a tree.

Your book is your tree and you're the god who created it. You were the only person present when the page was blank. Years ago, when I worked in an advertisng agency as a copywriter, I had to remind many an empty suit (an account executive) of this maxim.

A wit once remarked that a camel is an animal designed by a committee. So remember that committees of people don't (or shouldn't) write books. One person does. That's you. Editors suggest changes. Then, it is up to you as an author to measure the worth of those suggestions and act upon them.

Generally speaking, many of the changes my editors suggest make sense. I therefore diligently incorporate

most of their gentle suggestions into the final draft of a manuscript.

If I balk, my editor will often shrug and say, "Okay, Rob, it's your book."

Editors are friends. They are hardworking folk who want you to succeed. If you and your book fail, they fail.

Very few authors can edit their own stuff. I know I can't. Therefore, let your editor do his thing. He (or she) will weed your garden and separate the wheat from the tares. He'll keep what's sweet and cut what's sour.

A good editor tightens a book, hones a sharper edge on many a paragraph, and often helps in the consistency of your characterizations. He gives a manuscript polish. An editor adds little, because adding is not his job. He cuts. Most authors (including me) tend to overwrite. So let his blue pencil whack away and chop down a few of those golden phrases that so poetically say nothing. Allow him to tap the genius from your tree and let it flow.

Let's assume you are still an emerging author and you never have had a novel published. And then . . . BAM. You get a letter or a phone call from Harper & Row and an editor there tells you he's interested.

Listen well:

Be easy to work with. Be limber. Go along with what your editor suggests, at least at the start. Especially when the two of you get around to talking money.

I find editors and publishers to be honest. And I am a Vermonter, not easily impressed by city folks.

Accept the first offer and don't dicker. As you become famous, you can horse-trade a sweeter deal down the road. But as for now, follow this basic rule of salesmanship:

Shut up and take the money.

If you do both you and your editor will be happy. Publishers are not out to cheat you. They want you to prosper. Because they prosper only if you and your book do well.

Be flexible.

Just because your editor lives and works in New York does not necessarily mean that he is crude and stupid. So, instead of constantly telling your editor how much you know, listen to what *he* knows and is willing to share with you. Then *you* will know what both of you know, and you'll be twice as smart.

My editor at Knopf, Ash Green, suggested that I throw out one entire chapter of *Eagle Fur*.

"Cull it," he told me.

I culled it. (Only, however, after I hung up the phone and threw one heck of a creative tantrum and stuck pins in my Ash Green doll.) Later, in a fit of pique, I called him back, and gave him both barrels.

"Cut it?" I screamed. "It's the best chapter in the whole damn book!"

"No, it isn't."

"Is so."

"Isn't."

"What's wrong with it?"

"Rob, it doesn't say anything. It fails to move the book along."

In a resonant baritone, I read him a few of the chapter's more poetic passages, golden phrases all. Then, I added a few more personal comments to vent my opinions of his editorial ability as well as his intellect and ancestry.

He sighed. "Are you through?"

"Yes."

"Cut it."

We cut it. Threw it out. Discarded each and every golden phrase. Believe it or not, *Eagle Fur* survived the amputation and the book (as well as its paperback edition) did well.

But I still have that one typewritten chapter, and I plan to sneak all of those glib and golden phrases into manuscripts I send him in the future. Ash, in turn, will brutally scratch them out and then refuse to answer his phone. (But his doll will suffer.)

He was right. I was wrong.

Don't fret. Your editor will let you win a spat or two. Editors are good guys. So remember that the two of you are not mortal enemies. Both of you hold a single purpose: to make your book the best it can be. Tiffs are bound to ensue. Even about your *title*. Perhaps your editor stepped on a different thumbtack.

If, in the bickering, you lose . . . your book may win. Mine did.

I repeat: Your editor's prime function, in my opinion, is to *cut*. Painful though it may be to an author, when in doubt, throw it out. It makes sense to hearken to the folks who are working to make you richer. And you can always holler "Pearls before swine!" at him or some other dandy little artistic epithet.

But your temper is less useful than your editor.

Editors know things that authors don't know. I never truly know what I have written. Why? Because I'm too close to it, deep inside it, where I can't see the whole of the book. My editor can.

So he'll trim, buff, polish . . . and that's the easy part. His toughest job is handling the author's ire. My advice is to let your trainer train you.

Yet final decisions are yours alone. You were alone when the page was blank.

Life of a Salesman

You are *not* in literature.

You *are* in business.

If, once published, you want to fail as a businessman, here's how to do it:

Never appear in public. Stay home and lurk behind your typewriter. This will give you the opportunity to telephone your publisher twice a year (when the checks arrive) to complain that your royalties are puny.

Now, if starvation is what turns you on, if you're really into hunger, maintain an attitude of "I wrote it. You sell it" with your publisher.

My royalty checks are fat. Digits followed by lots of 0's.

Knowing that I am far from ever being the most gifted novelist at Doubleday, Knopf, and Little, Brown, I decided to be their best salesman.

All over the country trots Peck, speaking at schools, libraries, colleges, and in many a damp church basement. I keynote almost every month at state conferences of librarians, teachers, and reading specialists.

I talk to groups of men, women, and children.

Do you know *when* the best time is to sell a book? I do. It's right after you speak.

So wherever you go, take tons of books with you. I have

twenty-five books out and they are all in print. Why? Because I huckster them with shameless abandon.

There you stand, in front of a hundred eager listeners who want not just one of your books, but one of your *autographed* books. Sign a lot of books and you'll sign a lot of checks. Writing is not an art: It's a business. It's what you do for a living.

Americans are people who love to buy and sell goods. It is not government that feeds us, but our own sweaty hustle. So roll up your sleeves and wade in.

Agreed, it is hard work to arrive at where you are scheduled to speak and then have to lug in several weighty boxes of your wares. Worse yet, when nobody buys any and you have to carry all the books back out.

A good writer is a pack mule.

So hitch up. You'll soon have the bank balance of a tycoon and the arm of a Sumo wrestler.

Accept every invitation you get to speak. When the Sumpwater Methodist Church telephones to tell you that all eleven members of the Ladies Aid read your book and want you to speak, for free . . . go. And take a box of books with you.

Don't hide. If you do, those puny little royalty checks

will find you. So travel around our vast republic.

Being a frequent speaker rests you from the dull job of having to write every day. Meeting people and going places gives your brain input, to charge up your output. A writer has to feed the hopper to keep feeding the typewriter.

The secret of big checks is checking into many a musty motel. With baggage, boxes of books, and blisters. Maybe this will prove too lowly a task for a great writer like you. It ain't for me. Not all candlelight and gypsy violins, this being famous.

Getting rich is hard work.

I can't say for sure and for certain that "they loved me in Keokuk." Yet they sure loved me at Knopf, at Doubleday, and at Little, Brown; because I went to Kansas, Iowa, Illinois, and Ohio. And made thirty-three speeches in three weeks.

That adds up to thirty-three audiences of bored people who felt so sorry for me that they bought all my books. Oh, those beautiful empty boxes.

Now then, now that you're on the road, what do you do during your off-hours at that Ark City, Kansas, motel? I'll tell you what I did. Wrote a book. Started it in Kansas, added chapters in Iowa and Illinois, finished it in Sharonville, Ohio. Matter of fact, it happens to be the book you're reading right now.

Will you speak for free, or fee?

At the outset, you probably won't be offered the kind of honorarium (loot) that I command. So speak a freebie. Lots of them, until you polish your act and can deliver that speech while playing a harmonica upside down in a barrel of water. It doesn't matter what you talk about. Just be your entertaining self.

Never read your speech. And please do not shuffle 3x5 cards as if you're practicing to deal Faro at Vegas. Know in advance what you're going to say. If you don't know anything (without notes), then shut up and don't speak.

Warning: If you read your speech, people may think you dull and that your books are, too. And *never* read passages from your books. Unless you want to be boring. (Do you know the definition of a crashing bore? It's a man who was born in Texas, served in the Marines, and then went to Notre Dame.)

As you progress as a speaker, your fee will augment. Isn't that nifty? And, on top of that, you will also sell more books. And your publishers will grin. And want to publish your next book and send you out to Ark City to pitch it. You'll be in demand. Your picture will grace the pages of the Sumpwater Gazette. Local TV and radio talk-show people will beg to interview you and ask you deep and probing questions, like "What made you become a writer?"

Don't flinch.

Smile. Jingle the change in your pocket. And constantly cover up your face (on TV) by holding up your book. Throw it up in the air. Use it to crack the interviewer on the knee. Repeat the title in every sentence you say. Don't talk philosophy. *Talk product.* Procter & Gamble doesn't sell P&G. It sells Ivory soap.

Do not mention the book you're currently working on. Why? Because it is not in bookstores. Follow Peck's rule of effective publicity. I call it SWAT: Sell What's Available Today. Avoid the book that's coming out next year. Sell the book that you're waving at the camera.

Lift weights. Jog.

You'll need those muscles to tote boxes of books along the dingy halls of distant motels. And for running with them through airports. I once jumped over O.J. Simpson.

It's a pain, and it's a pleasure. And it takes all the hurry and hustle you can muster. That's what being a famous author is all about. Touting and toting.

The life of a salesman.

How to Feed a Dinosaur

See that one-eyed box in your den?

You call it your TV and it has become a household pet. What do you feed it? Or for that matter, what does it eat?

It eats words.

Somebody, somewhere, has to write all those scripts in order for them to be produced into TV shows. Why not you?

You're as observant as a good writer ought to be, and you've already noticed that lots of television programs are just plain lousy. Complete with canned laughter dubbed in to follow each unfunny joke.

Never gripe about TV quality. Sit down and dream up some fresh stuff, a show that is unusual, unique, and *better*.

Here's how to start:

Perhaps, if you write to the program director at any TV network he just might, at your request, send you old *scripts* and *treatments* of exciting television shows.

Or, your public library could help. Librarians are savvy folks and have aided me aplenty with my books.

Now let's say that you have created an idea for a TV series, but you don't know how to present it. Study both the scripts and treatments of other shows . . . for

structure, not for content. So the format that you finally present looks professional. In style.

Send your outline (treatment) to the program director, along with a sample script of a single half-hour episode. Plus several other ideas for future episodes, so that the show is not just a one-shot, but a sustained series.

Your *treatment* (not a script) should indicate:

1. Where the action takes place.

2. Who the characters are.

3. What they do. (Are they cops, doctors, soldiers, airline hostesses, teachers, merchants, Indians, cowboys, trappers, skin divers, or kids?)

A *treatment is structure,* not execution.

Your sample script, however, gives the program director an idea of how your show will look on a TV screen. One episode.

When you write your script, please time it. Trim it. Clock your action close to twenty-seven minutes.

Also, within those twenty-seven minutes, write a trio of three nine-minute segments (acts). These will allow time in between for station breaks, and commercials that tout new improved Glunko with K-34.

Take notes when you watch TV.

Check a newspaper to find out which television shows capture, week after week, the largest viewing audience. Then try to determine why. I can't. Maybe you can.

Be original.

If evenings are presently glutted with cop-crime shows, then don't submit just one more carbon copy. Fads die.

Watching prime-time (evening) shows is not your only helpmate. Concentrate, if you please, on some of the old reruns, TV shows of yesteryear that still survive on the air in the mornings, afternoons, early evenings.

Allow me to suggest:

The Dick VanDyke Show

I Love Lucy.

The Honeymooners.

Hogan's Heroes.

The Odd Couple.

The Beverly Hillbillies.

Don't ignore the long-in-the-tooth sitcom (situation comedy) merely because it is an oldie in black and white. In fact, if it is aired in BW, chances are this relic had some magic and a unique quality that an audience liked. It was, in its day, fresh. Not a copy.

If the old show continues to endure today, still on the air in syndication, see if you can figure out why. It may appear black and white to you; but to some writer, it's gold and silver, and trips to the bank.

And don't be aloof to prime-time programs.

Take note of what's on the air so that you are aware of what type of show is not being telecast. And then be original.

Important note: Even if you have no plans to write for TV, watch it anyhow. Television is actually a form of fiction, and there is much for you to learn if you approach it as scholar instead of just another bored viewer.

I believe that the most critical lesson that you will learn

from TV is the art of *characterization*. This is the guts of fiction. So also pay attention to the casting of TV commercials as well as the programs. Note, in each commercial, how *character* has to be established instantaneously.

Study carefully the characters in one show. The variety of personalities.

To wit, "The Beverly Hillbillies."

Jed, Jethro and Elly Mae, Granny, the banker and his gaunt secretary. They were not all of a kind. They were variety. Together they blended into a delightful recipe of varied ingredients.

One more thing. Jed and his family were *not* residing in their expected locale, a shack nestled back in the rural hills. Instead, they were living out of place, monkeys on the moon, bringing with them the wit and wisdom of down-home life and logic. An odd coupling.

Jed was the father, the patriarch, wise and kind and respected by the two youngsters, Jethro and Elly Mae. Jed and Granny were the revered elders who stood for what is wholesome, holding the Clampett family together.

They were different but not dumb.

Much of the humor of TBH sprouted from an urban problem solved by rural wisdom. Or a city-slicker ruse foiled by up-country sense, or elixir.

No fast-talking con artist could quite snatch Jed's fortune out of his blue jeans. Why not? Because the audience wouldn't have sat still for it. Jed represented the noble father that so many people perhaps wished they had. Spiritually, every American is a farmer. The mass audience will root for a Jed in every race. We holler for the hick, from Abraham Lincoln to Abner Yokum.

So, watch TV, and be aware of what America is now watching.

For two reasons: One, your fiction may prosper if you study the video fiction of other writers. Two, you may conclude that your TV set spews forth a lot of pap, and that you can do better.

Somebody has to write for TV. That hungry box in your parlor has an appetite that would make a Tyrannosaurus rex look like Heidi.

Remember that so much light comedy is based on matter out of place. Hillbillies in Beverly Hills. Mork from Ork in Boulder, Colorado. Gilligan's Island. So jerk somebody out of his usual environs and transplant him on foreign turf.

Television, on its diet of mediocrity, is hungry for the unusual situation. An odd coupling. Strange bedfellows. Ask yourself . . . what has *not* been done? Which events did you attend in real life that have been ignored by the tube?

If all the networks refuse your idea, prove to them and to yourself how wrong they are. Write your idea into a book. But try the networks first. Who knows?

In writing for television, don't worry even one second about the quality of your work. TV never heard of quality. It is, instead, totally a *numbers game*.

Broadcasting executives are not concerned with literary quality. They want to know how big (numbers) an audience it will pull. And also, the amount (numbers) of dollars that advertisers will pay for spots. So, don't fret about whether you write well. Just do your homework, write fresh material and you'll make it on television.

There is another, secondary advantage to TV writing. In the business world, I came up via broadcast, *not print*. This, I feel, has contributed greatly to my fame and fortune. Broadcast people can write, cast, shoot, and air a "Mork and Mindy" segment while print editors at publishing houses are bickering about whether a comma should be a colon.

TV is starving for your creative genius.

Feed it.

The Vanilla People

Who buys books?

The answer to that question is . . . just about everybody. John, Marsha, Aunt Mildred in Topeka—everybody.

Book clubs abound. Folks are buying paperbacks like never before, and they don't sell for a quarter anymore. Many of today's paperbacks sell for several dollars each. Bookstores are no longer little mom and pop holes-in-the-wall, but part of big chains. Bookstores are big business.

Emerging writers think, "You have to put sex in a novel or it just won't sell."

Wrong.

Most "sexy" passages are a bore. They seem to be written by the people at factories who list the steps used to assemble toys: "Insert wingnut F into cam device C, making sure that widget K is first firmly locked around the gizmo. . . ."

Ho hum.

Am I going to pay money to read *that*? Not me.

Remember that a writer, a good one, is also an artist. And the duty of art, or rather, the *privilege* of art, is to uplift and not degrade.

Write a book you're proud of.

And when folks read it, let them feel finer and cleaner and stronger for so doing. Don't make them feel, when they close your book, that they want to go gargle. Or wash.

As I write the final chapter to this book, I am fifty-one years old. And I have come to a few conclusions—idle rambles—that I shall now share with you.

I've concluded that the values in my life that I treasure most are *corny*. Singing in a barbershop quartet, playing ragtime piano, hearing my kids laugh, watching my wife brush her hair. Seeing our cat, Sarah, close her eyes when she lies on my chest and I caress her.

Things that I want to write about are often tender touchings of tough people. Folks that I vividly remember are the men and women with whom I worked. Rather than played. Work is more sacred than love.

I'd prefer to be remembered not as a great lover or a fantastic athlete or a rich author, but rather as a gentleman. Because true gentility takes more guts than does heroics.

In a modest way, I want to fight big government, and cheer for little people who oppose it. For an example, read *Justice Lion*, a courtroom novel that takes place in Vermont in 1923, during Prohibition.

In my opinion, America needs less law and more referenda. As to lawyers, I believe they ought not to monopolize Congress and federal bureaus. I'm not sure whether judges first have to be lawyers. I believe that lawyers should practice the law but not determine what the law will be.

People who do hard work talk more sense to me than people who don't.

I believe in mercy. Being merciful to potential victims of crimes, you and me, rather than wasting mercy on criminals and louts.

I read the Holy Bible.

What I don't believe in is "the word of God." I accept God's rain and rainbow, God's leaf and tree. But if you tell me that God spoke words and wrote the Bible, I'm changing my pew.

I enjoy movies in which cop cars crash.

Morality is acreage per head.

Many intellectuals I know neither read nor write. And some of the most moral men cook their own corn into whiskey. (My father referred to such activity as moonlight farming.)

Of the talents and opinions and emotions that I have been given, my temper is the least useful.

Every father and son should raise a pig, and slaughter it together, so that both man and boy will forever know who and what they are.

A child's first musical instrument should be a ukulele because it so simply embraces the prime laws of melody, harmony, and rhythm.

My favorite composer is Scott Joplin.

Our US Supreme Court does not determine supreme law, which can only be enacted by God and practiced by Nature.

God is female. In the most rudimentary syllogism of Aristotelian logic: God is the giver of life. A giver of life is female. Ergo, God is female.

Haven Peck, my father, told me that we Vermonters had two talents: We could turn grass into milk, and corn into hogs. I now believe that we Americans must develop a third talent: that being, to turn corn into motor fuel.

Work spurs the mind more than books.

An author (to get rich) must be a showman. In the world of book hustling, I am Liberace.

Miss Kelly was my only teacher for six years. I believe that I learned more in those six years I sat in a dirtroad one-room Vermont schoolhouse than either of my children will learn inside a million-dollar edifice.

Having been a farmer, a soldier, a lumberjack, a paper mill worker, and a football player . . . I think the hardest job in the world is being a father or mother.

Strong men are the most gentle. It is only the weaklings who slap people around.

Winners always smile. Losers grumble, frown, swear, smash tennis racquets, throw golf clubs and tantrums. No one remembers the score. Everyone remembers whether or not you were a lady or a gentleman.

Our planet, earth, is female. Plant seed into her and she will bear fruit. The wind, which carries pollen, is male.

All of the principal problems on our planet earth stem from a present excess of human population.

Most of all, I am unsure that any of my beliefs are correct. I want no one to agree with me, but rather to respect my right to a conflicting opinion.

I do not want you to *obey* the rules in this book but merely to consider them.

Write your book to an audience of Vanilla People. Not to the hip crowd. Most of us are square. (We hate to admit it.) We are a nation of work and prayer, Lawrence Welk and Hee Haw, and a hunk of Velveeta on a Ritz cracker.

Our fantasies swing, but our lifestyle is Puritan and Pilgrim.

More than any other people on earth, we Americans are the Vanilla People. We drudge and we dream. Don't tell me, please, that there is no Santa, no Easter Bunny, no Tooth Fairy, and no American Way of Life.

Write for the Vanilla People and you'll never starve. In fact, you'll get rich. But don't wish for apples.

Grow strong trees.

Index

Other Writer's Digest Books

Artist's Market, 540 pp. $11.95
Beginning Writer's Answer Book, 264 pp. $8.95
Cartoonist's and Gag Writer's Handbook, (paper), 157 pp. $8.95
Complete Guide to Marketing Magazine Articles, 248 pp. $8.95
Confession Writer's Handbook, 200 pp. $8.95
Craft of Interviewing, 244 pp. $9.95
Craftworker's Market, 696 pp. $12.95
Creative Writer, 416 pp. $8.95
Guide to Greeting Card Writing, 256 pp. $10.95
Guide to Writing History, 258 pp. $8.50
Handbook of Short Story Writing, 238 pp. $9.95
How to Be a Successful Housewife/Writer, 254 pp. $10.95
How to Write Short Stories that Sell, 228 pp. $9.95
How You Can Make $20,000 a Year Writing: No Matter Where You Live, 270 pp. (cloth) $10.95; (paper) $6.95
Jobs For Writers, 256 pp. $10.95
Law and the Writer, 240 pp. $9.95
Magazine Writing: The Inside Angle, 256 pp. $10.95
Magazine Writing Today, 220 pp. $9.95
Make Every Word Count, 256 pp. $10.95
Mystery Writer's Handbook, 273 pp. $8.95
1001 Article Ideas, 270 pp. $10.95
One Way to Write Your Novel, 138 pp. $8.95
Photographer's Market, 640 pp. $12.95
The Poet and the Poem, 399 pp. $11.95
Poet's Handbook, 256 pp. $10.95
Profitable Freelancing, 256 pp. $10.95
Scriptwriter's Handbook, 256 pp. $10.95
Secrets of Successful Fiction, 140 pp. $8.95
Sell Copy, 205 pp. $11.95
Songwriter's Market, 504 pp. $11.95
Stalking the Feature Story, 310 pp. $9.95
Successful Outdoor Writing, 244 pp. $11.95
Travel Writer's Handbook, 288 pp. $11.95
Treasury of Tips for Writers, 174 pp. $7.95
Writer's Market, 936 pp. $15.95
Writer's Resource Guide, 488 pp. $12.95
Writing and Selling Non-Fiction, 317 pp. $10.95
Writing and Selling Science Fiction, 191 pp. $8.95
Writing for Children & Teenagers, 269 pp. $9.95
Writing for Regional Publications, 203 pp. $11.95
Writing the Novel: From Plot to Print, 197 pp. $10.95
Writing Popular Fiction, 232 pp. $8.95

To order directly from the publisher, include $1.25 postage and handling for 1-2 books; for 3 or more books, include an additional 25¢ for each book. Allow 30 days for delivery.

For a current catalog of books for writers, write to Department B, **Writer's Digest Books, 9933 Alliance Road, Cincinnati OH 45242**

Prices subject to change without notice.